The Realized Idiot

If you want to make sure that a tradition will keep its effectiveness than develop it.
A Chinese Feng-shui master

Bruno Martin

The Realized Idiot

*The Artful Psychology of G. I. Gurdjieff
and the "Science of Idiotism"*

In grateful acknowledgement to my mentor John G. Bennett (1897-1974)

© 2008 Original Version, Germany, by Bruno Martin
© 2008/2015 English/American translation by Bruno Martin
Translated from German by Bruno Martin, edited by Pippa Arend and
Mike Krochmal

© 2007 Tarot deck "Tarot of Marseille" by Lo Scarabeo, Turin. Printing
permission by Königsfurt Verlag. www.koenigsfurt.com

Layout: Bruno Martin
Cover-title and design by Nana Nauwald © 2008
Layout Cover: Sabine Motta

Printing and Publisher: Books on Demand, Norderstedt, Germany

Information to Gurdjieff and Bruno Martin (only in German):
www.gurdjieff-work.de

ISBN 978-3-7347-7450-03

Contents

"There are twenty-one gradations of 'Idiots' – of identity, of kinds of beings. This gives you the picture of the going out and the returning, but it also adds something more, which is very important, and that is that there can be a kind of false returning, a returning which has not got the potential for totality. This is what Gurdjieff was anxious to get over to people with his Science of Idiotism: that every kind of effort produces an integrative effect – a soul is made whenever there is an act of decision – something is integrated. But integration is not enough. Integration has to be such that it can reach completion."

John G. Bennett, After-Lunch Discussion, unpublished

Foreword

In contemporary language, the word "idiot" means "fool". But the Greeks had a very different meaning. Their word, *idiotes*, referred to a private or simple man, derived from the word *idios*, which means to be of one's own, particular or special. G. I. Gurdjieff (1866-1949)[1] used it in the sense of "being oneself", because a man who is truly himself can appear foolish, though only to those who actually *are* foolish - those whose perceptions are clouded by judgment. To be declared an "Idiot", then, is a compliment of the highest degree - it means that one is not sharing the common illusions which sedate us all, but rather has found his or her private, unique individuality. In the words of John G. Bennett (1897-1974), who studied with Gurdjieff, "Everyone who decides to work on himself is an idiot in both meanings. The wise know that he is seeking reality. The foolish think he has taken leave of his senses."[2]

As today the term "idiot" is only used in a humiliating or ignominious sense, I pondered for a while if I can also use it in its original meaning today. I came to the conclusion that it might be correct to use it, because today many people are not willing to "look deeper" and do not want to question general human traits. The "Science of Idiotism" therefore puts out a challenge for those who are striving to get to the bottom of their own being – for those who want to become an Idiot in the original sense and step up the "ladder of reason" as Gurdjieff puts it.

For those who know little or nothing about Gurdjieff - the teacher of wisdom who taught in France from 1922 until his death - I have included some of the basics of his psychology in this book. If you want to study his teachings in full, you should read the foremost work of his outstanding pupil Pjotr D. Ouspensky, titled *In Search of the Miraculous*. The books and works of John G. Bennett also helped me very much in clarifying this teaching. Furthermore, among Bennett's great merits are that he developed many of Gurdjieff's ideas for our time, and that he incorporated new insights.

The first time I took part in a "ritual meal" with the "Toasts to the Idiots" in the tradition of Gurdjieff was at the beginning of the 1970s and under the leadership of John G. Bennett. At that time, I visited his "Academy for Continuous Education" (today it could be translated into "life long learning"). This ritual impressed me so much that many years later, when I had established own work groups, I started to conduct this ritual myself. And with time I learned more and more about "idiotic psychology", and started to research it more deeply.

As I couldn't have been at Gurdjieffs meals because of my age, and was merely able to study the reports and literature about him and his methods of teaching, it was necessary in many cases for me to intuit what he meant with his many cryptic and symbolic expressions, so that I could develop a certain understanding about "Idiots". So please forgive me if I didn't get it quite "right". But then again, what exactly is "right"? As John G. Bennett once stated, it is never possible for us to see the whole truth, only aspects of it. Therefore what is right for somebody might be completely wrong for another person – although at the same time, it may be "right" in the context of the whole, which we are unable to conceive completely.

It would also have been possible for me to delve much more deeply into the historical and oral tradition of people who wrote down everything that Gurdjieff said. But that would be history, and my undertaking here is not present a historical study. If the teaching about the "Science of the Idiots" contains some timeless insights, then we have to look for that in the sense of the Zen-master Basho, who once put it this way: "Don't look for the wisdom of the old, look for that which they have sought for themselves." So, my approach is neither academic nor intellectual. It's intuitive and creative, but of course, I am making use of material I have researched. It also developed out of many ritual meals I facilitated over some years with many people in Germany and Italy, and also of my practical and theoretical work with Gurdjieff's and Bennett's teachings over 40 years - both alone and in groups.

My aim with this book is to recover the "lost" psychology which Gurdjieff used extensively in his teachings and during many ritual meals he conducted with his students. "Psychology should be an art", Gurdjieff said. "Psychology can never be just a science." In fact, the psyche of a person only can be understood intuitively. It is also necessary to have long years of experience with oneself and other people. The artfulness of Gurdjieff's psychology consists of the "pictures" or metaphors which he designed to illustrate special traits of humans. And because we can understand these metaphor types much more easily than intellectual descriptions or theoretical categories, they appear to be much more effective.

According to all sources which I consulted, Gurdjieff had already commenced this mode of teaching during his time at the Prieuré in the 1920s, and as the reports indicate, he carried out these rituals nearly every day during his time in Paris - especially in the 1940s. Most of the people who were with him are now dead, or if they are still alive, they refuse to speak about this topic with anybody who is an "outsider" to them, either because that person had not been with Gurdjieff, or even because they had been a pupil of the "renegade" Mr. John G. Bennett (as I was).

But this is of no importance. There are reports about Gurdjieff's naming and interpreting the various "idiots". And I discovered a key for the better interpretation of his cryptic representations: in using one of the oldest decks of Tarot cards (namely "Tarot of Marseilles") it was possible for me to reconstruct the meaning of most of the "idiots" – you will find more detailed explanations in chapter 4. Although most "Gurdjieff-followers" will not agree with this parallelism, you will see that both teachings are comparable or even compatible – but only in the way I use the sequence of the Tarot, which is the reverse of the usual. Of course, in this little book, it has not been possible for me to go into the deeper meaning of the Tarot itself (although in the appendix you'll find some background of its origins), as I wanted to concentrate on Gurdjieff's psychology, and not on becoming involved with a subject which deserves to be examined much more thoroughly. It was sufficient for me that with the use of these pictures, I obtained some assistance in understanding the different idiot types.

If you think that there is important information missing from this book, or that some interpretation has gone astray completely, then please let me know. We may be able to add or alter material in the next print run, or somebody can create an internet blog for this, if enough interesting additions and corrections are received. I hope that you will find this lecture entertaining, and that this book will add something valuable to your existing wisdom!

Bruno Martin

A note to the teaching stories I use: Many of my stories come from the Zen- or Sufi-traditions. I have recast them in accordance with my understanding of their meaning, and have modified them in some cases, to facilitate better understanding.[3] Teaching stories are a means of connecting with our right brain wisdom, with intuition and creative insight, and in many cases they have different meanings on different levels. Gurdjieff himself used this technique extensively in his work *Beelzebub's Tales to his Grandson.*

1. Why I Want to Become an Idiot

"Life is only real then, when 'I am'."
G.I. Gurdjieff

In *In Search of the Miraculous*, Pjotr D. Ouspensky's book which is a chronicle of G.I. Gurdjieff's early teachings, Gurdjieff, is reported to have emphasized that his teaching is called the *Fourth Way* because it succeeds the traditional three ways – that of the fakir (body work / matter), the monk (feeling work / soul) and the yogi (intellectual work / spirit). The Fourth Way is said to be the "way of the sly man" because it is more than a mere synthesis; it is a higher, comprehensive, and more intelligent way of working towards one's inner development.

Not to be taken lightly, this numerical symbolism can be rich in content and multifold in meaning, which is why Gurdjieff valued and widely implemented its use. Whether in the naming of this psychology, The Fourth Way, or his use of "geometric idiots" in the Idiot Typology (explained in detail in Chapter Four), Gurdjieff used numbers as well as the emotional language of symbolism to convey psychological and spiritual ideas. For example, Gurdjieff used the symbols of the dyad, triad and tetrad as a metaphor of man's evolution, from mechanical man (the dyad) to harmonious man, shown in the balance of the square. Taking this idea a step further, when a square has a fifth point placed in the center, and raised to form a pyramid, this is an excellent representation of man reaching another dimension, discovering his "quintessence". Gurdjieff's Fourth Way is about the discovery of this internal curiosity, our Individuality, and the "Science of Idiotism" was a tool which he developed to help with the objective observation of the self which is needed to make this discovery. Ouspensky wrote: "The transmission of the meanings of symbols to a man who has not reached an understanding of them in himself is impossible." [4]

To better understand the ladder of Gurdjieff's "Idiot Typology", and his teaching in general, we should know that he emerged from the tradition of the eastern masters, specifically the "Masters of the Moment". Gurdjieff's own spiritual path took him on long journeys through Eastern Europe, Central Asia and North Africa - through studies of many traditional esoteric teachings and much of the scientific knowledge available at his time. He acquired a tremendous body of knowledge and techniques, as well as a deep understanding of their use and applicability. One of the critical influences on his teaching was the tradition of the *School of the Moment*, which he learned from the *Masters of Wisdom* in Turkistan.[5] "Gurdjieff brought their teaching and converted it into a practical way of life for the modern world, not only for individuals, but for the whole of humanity."[6]

In the same way that many Zen monks intentionally broke free from formalized teachings, branching off instead into the "Way of the Crazy Clouds"[7], Gurdjieff did not remain in any specific school, seeking instead to explore all of the esoteric, philosophic and scientific knowledge of the day. In fact, in reference to the core of his teachings, Gurdjieff gave credit to the "Sarmoun Brotherhood". "Sarmoun" can be translated as "bees", in other words, "that which gathers honey from many flowers". However, more than a mere synthesis of Sufism, Tibetan Buddhism, Esoteric Christianity, and Western psychology, among others, he wrought his findings into a unique form, the tone of which resonates with the deepest quest for Reality.

In a *School of the Moment*, emphasis is placed on the realization of the totality of one's potential at any given moment, through deep awareness of the moment. This is based on the idea that reality is not static, nothing is fixed, and infinite possibilities abound, an idea which is corroborated by quantum physics -

"vibrating wave fields" lie at the very core of matter, and the behavior of these fields is wildly erratic and completely uncertain. In the Fourth Way, great deference is given to the idea of the mutable nature of our very existence, and the idea that spiritual training *must* reflect this uncertainty. In a School of the Moment, preconceived forms and dogmas are seldom used, but instead more emphasis is placed on spontaneous teachings inspired by the moment. A renowned Sufi was asked: "Why do you tolerate thoughtless and impulsive questions?" He laughed and said, "In order for all of us to have the benefit of becoming acquainted with questions such as you have just presented."

All great masters know that the knowledge of the "Laws of the Universe" is not the domain of any particular spiritual tradition or teaching. The task G. I. Gurdjieff set for himself, however, was to transmit a modern, practical way of penetrating one's real self, and of tuning into the underlying spiritual force (or *baraka*, blessing, as the Sufi name it) of the Universe through direct attention to, and transformation of, the self.

Such a teaching must be able to contain paradoxes - being at once able to encompass timeless principles, while also being the lens that brings the present moment into exacting focus. In Kendo, the Japanese art of sword fighting, students learn to embody this paradox – they learn to be supremely aware of the moment, in all its possibilities, yet attached to nothing. "When the mind lingers upon any kind of object, be it the sword of the opponent or the opponent himself, his own sword, his own body, his action which he calls upon as a defense or to attack, he is in every case overcome and conquered. The contrast between subject and object must be overcome. The assault and the defense must become one thing."[8] The goal of this training is utter awareness and ability to act, to be the spontaneous wave field at the core of the moment. In this heightened and receptive state, a person experiences a freedom from the trappings of everything which is not truly one's own, including the past and present, which only serve to bind and distract. In parable form: A millipede was going contentedly on his way when he was asked, "How do you manage to coordinate all the movements of your thousand feet?" He thought this over for a bit and was thereupon no longer able to move.

While the body is always in the moment, the mind - subject to all sorts of fantasies and attachments - frequently is not. So to think too much about the moment, one ironically misses it entirely. In other words, when looking for anything as fine in substance and as fleeting as a moment, think with anything but the head, which is really much too slow and ill-suited to the task. Imagine a language that isn't accessed through the intellect. The body, and especially the emotions, are much quicker receivers of impressions and can therefore assess any given moment in a way that the head cannot even conceive.

As a true Master of the Moment, Gurdjieff continuously researched and experimented with new exercises, methods and techniques to develop the capacities for attention directed to self-observation. He developed "alchemical" exercises to transform inner energies, explored breathing techniques and, of course, the ever-present practical work.[9] He observed that humans are composed of separate functions, or centers, and each of these is controlled by a distinct "brain". In our current state of development they are not in sync with each other, and one often tries to do the work of another. This causes all sorts of imbalance and chaos in our perceptions and experience of the world. Through his exercises, students were taught to observe and eventually correct the imbalances of these different "brains" or "functions". It is only through the *harmonious* development of Man that "Real I" can emerge. As described by Ouspensky, the aim is the development of the "human machine" and the enrichment of being with a new and unaccustomed functioning.

In Gurdjieff's teaching a human being has basically three centers (moving, feeling, and intellect), in another version there are seven centers, if you divide the body or moving part into the moving, the instinctive, and the sex. The feeling part does have an emotional and a "higher emotional" part as well as the intellectual center does have a normal and "higher intellectual" part. If you know about the chakras then these centers can be compared with these. So this throws another light on the work of the harmonious development of the centers whereby is not meant to enhance the normal brain functions but the "inner qualities" of the spiritual being. The predominant development of any one center at the expense of the others produces an extremely one-sided type of man, incapable of further development. And on a functional side this process has to do with transformation of lower energies into higher.[10]

Of particular importance in this quest for harmonious balance of the functions was Gurdjieff's use of his "holy gymnastics", a series of dances and moving exercises known collectively as the *Movements*. These dances integrated various parts of the body, various numbers of people (moving in various ways), various specific emotions to be rendered at various specific moments, various spoken or thought word and/or number sequences, and various parts of the body to be sensed at various times, all variously coordinated or not coordinated with the rhythm of the music. The undeniable complexity of certain Movements causes either deep despair or a "Zen of Sudden Enlightenment", to reference the experience of the Kendo student, in which one suddenly acts from a profound awareness of the moment, allowing action to simply flow spontaneously through you, in spite of you, in conjunction with you. You become a vessel with 1000 feet.

As a man, Gurdjieff had a profound effect on those around him. He was both lauded and criticized, as people of great stature generally are. He received considerable attention (both positive and negative) for his actions and words, and specifically for his work in the *Institute for the Harmonious Development of Man*[11], which he opened in Fontainebleau, France, in the early 1920's. The lives of the people with whom he worked were profoundly changed, and many went on to teach this Work, eventually creating a network of thousands of students of the Fourth Way. Sixty-six years after his death, we can see the depth of the effect that his teachings have had on modern psychology and spirituality throughout the world. One can see his influence, for example, in the widespread use of the *Enneagram* (a triangle and a hexagon, conjoined within a circle) that he introduced in 1915, even though current use of this diagram typically ties it to other uses and typologies not originated by him. Also, we see his lasting effect in the sheer volume of books published by his students and students of his students, and beyond.

Gurdjieff's own typology, the "Idiot Typology" and the subject of this book, has been little taught and remains generally unknown to most people. One reason is due ironically to a sort of Gurdjieff-worship; that it was *his* ritual. Another reason that it fell into relative obscurity lies in the inherent problem of conveying any of the ideas in a School of the Moment: that the method of transmission is defunct as soon as the moment has passed. Gurdjieff offered a unique countermeasure to this problem of translation by use of the "encrypted language" of his books and teachings (we'll venture to read a passage in upcoming chapters). It was either a clever tool or the fact that English was not his first language, or perhaps both, that kept his students and generations after continually searching for the real meaning of his cryptic tongue. That issue aside, his books are written in such a difficult manner, and often with such new and unfamiliar terminology, that little can be gained by trying to learn with "thinking center" alone. One must dive in, with the whole of one's entirety and understanding, making any interpretation of his ideas current by dint of the sheer effort of understanding in the moment. He explained: "There is no mystery whatsoever. But the acquisition or transmission of true knowledge demands great labor and great effort both of him who receives and of him who gives.... Knowledge cannot come to people without effort on their own part. They understand this very well in connection with ordinary knowledge, but in the case of great knowledge, when they admit the possibility of its existence, they find it possible to expect something different."[12]

In the tradition of Zen-Buddhism, which always leaves something incomplete, Gurdjieff was a Samurai – a Zen-Master[13]. Like the ink-drawn circle with an open gap, and like the paradoxical image of "the sound of one hand clapping", the way he presented his ideas was spontaneous, non-linear and left one to find one's own conclusions. Some ideas were left unfinished; others were allowed to evolve into new forms or with new terminology. "He never gave anything in a finished form. He always gave only beginnings of ideas, leaving it to his pupils to work them out. He never bothered about terminology and nomenclature, taking the first words that occurred to him and fitting them to his purpose..."[14] His aim was to present to his pupils and the readers of his books the task of completing an idea (or to some, the idea of completing a task!) - to study, to discover and to understand, individually, the consequence and value of these teachings. Bennett lamented, "He took every opportunity to tell me that I was a disappointment to him... I had done my best to follow his guidance and instructions. I had failed in *understanding* what was required, and in Gurdjieff's method this is the worst sin. Anyone can do what they understand, but not to understand is like the sin against the Holy Ghost which cannot be forgiven in this world or the next..."[15]

Ouspensky describes their work together in St. Petersburg in 1916, and complains that he did not understand everything about the way these meetings were arranged. It seemed to him that G. was making much of it unnecessarily difficult. For instance, "he seldom allowed me to fix a meeting beforehand..." It could happen that Gurdjieff said to him: "Why not have a meeting tonight?" He then should ring up those who wanted to come and tell them, where to meet. The reason was not to make it *easy* for people to become acquainted with his ideas. One had to make a certain effort to value the ideas.[16] Of course – if you look at Moscow today with its 12 Millions inhabitants (I just have been there); or New York or London – you cannot make such appointments in so short a time. This also points to the meaning of "School of the Moment": you also have to do things which fit into the existing environment and the people's mental and societal circumstances.

All great Masters, with few exceptions, have used the incalculable experiences provided by daily life for the training of their students. While inner exercises, alone or in a group, serve invaluably to strengthen and transform (without which there is no growth), the intrinsic work happens within the normal circumstances of life. The teacher's actions may seem paradoxical or without reason, but they have the intention of creating situations (tense or joyous – it doesn't matter) from which to learn. From the outside, the resulting behavior of either the student or the teacher may seem odd. Bennett reports, "Sometimes young women would come to Paris to visit Gurdjieff. He would flirt outrageously with them, and invite them to come back to the flat late at night when everyone had gone. Often thinking that this was some kind of mysterious test, or just frankly curious, they would go. In all cases that I heard of, Gurdjieff would open the door, look astonished and say: 'Why you come now?' give them a handful of sweets and send them away."[17]

Having no formal method or fixed doctrines, a School of the Moment, by definition, responds to the demands/needs of the moment. It must take advantage of, or even exacerbate, the frustrations and upsets of daily life, valuing them as the raw material for psychological transformation. In such a school, things are rarely what they seem and every event is an opportunity. In every situation the students are presented with new and unexpected challenges, the goal of which is to train the dual qualities of alertness and inner flexibility. When carpooling, for an example, Gurdjieff often left earlier than the agreed upon time. Bennett recalls, "We set out in three car loads, and others went by train to join us at Vichy... Unless you knew this trick, you were liable to arrive punctually and find the party had left half an hour earlier."[18]

In another example, in Gurdjieff's training centre at the Prieuré in Fontainebleau, there was a student with whom nobody could get along. He was irritable, unkempt, uncooperative and, according to Gurdjieff, invaluable. To the great relief of the other students, he eventually departed. Gurdjieff immediately implored him to come back, eventually having to offer a financial incentive. When the other students heard of this, uproar broke out, but Gurdjieff laughed and explained, "This man is for you what yeast is for bread. If he were not here, you would never learn what rage, irascibility, patience and mercy are. For this reason, you must pay me money for the stay and I will pay him, thereby you can learn something." In Gurdjieff's system, this vital factor for growth was called "friction", and Gurdjieff encouraged seeing the *totality* of a situation as a way of extracting usefulness and meaning. As we venture in later chapters to the study of Idiotism, we will find the capacity for observing subtleties in the intense environment of a ritual dinner, or in your daily life, to be central to our work.

As Masters of the Moment, it is not of much concern to Zen Masters that their students meditate for days on end or solve koans (paradoxical doctrines), but rather to remain alert and responsive to the moment, allowing for decisions to be made in one moment that would not be made in the next. To illustrate:

There was a Zen Master in whose room the rain would come in through a leaky roof. He called for his monks and asked that they bring him something whereby the tatami (straw mats) could be kept dry. One of them, without a moment's hesitation, brought a bamboo basket while the others searched all over for a barrel. The Master, as it is written, was overjoyed with the monk who had brought the basket.

Even though the bamboo basket wasn't waterproof, this monk's actions had expressed the idea of "non-discrimination", of acting, right or wrong, spontaneously in the moment. This "Zen spirit" is also seen in Zen art: "No hesitation is allowed, no erasing, no tracing, no retouching, no redesign. Once drawn, the lines are once and for always firm. The inspiration is something spontaneous, absolute, instantaneous..."[19] The value is action, not pondering.

Attention and action are properties of the will of the "Real I". How attention can be concentrated is one of the secrets of this teaching. A useful tool is self-observation, which allows the student to see by what he or she is distracted, with what he or she is identified. For this reason, certain teaching situations are capable of causing a lot of friction, because students are constantly confronted by their identifications. This friction helps to build up energy, however - a necessary ingredient in the transformation of lead into gold. The beauty of self-observation is that every experience can be observed, even the effort toward, or failure of, this practice. If we are confronted with determining which sort of idiot we are, we easily roll down the hill of identification, thinking ourselves 'kind' and therefore obviously a Compassionate Idiot, or terribly smart and energetic, and so perhaps one of the Geometric Idiots (but certainly not a Pretending Idiot!). Fortunately however, the Idiot Typology doesn't create any opportunity to find any more or less "Pleasant Idiot" – none escape complete idiocy! Gurdjieff's Idiot Typology consists of 21 types of Idiots, and provides a specific context from which to self-observe. It is a tool. It suggests certain questions, such as "What kind of Idiot am I?" "Have I done enough in life to warrant Idiocy?" "Which Idiot would I like to be?" "Which Idiot am I more likely to be?" "Who am I right now (posture, mood, habit, presentation, etc)?" It is easy to lose objectivity, falling prey to our pre-fabricated pictures of ourselves.

Gurdjieff used the ritual meal, "The Feast of the Idiots" to share this "Science of Idiotism". These tended to be quite intense affairs in which participants were involved in exercises of attention and self-observation. Rina Hands remembers, "There was a very solemn moment during dinner. The director gave the toast to Hopeless Idiots. Mr. Gurdjieff stopped him and said he was not thinking about what he was saying. He must think about what he said, when he said 'perish like dogs' he must realize the horror of it. The young man then repeated the toast and I thought he was going to cry with the realization. Then Mr. Gurdjieff said: 'Good, now you understand,' and gave him a croissant to take home for his breakfast. He then said we must remember this toast. Now he saw that we were beginning to smell what it means, so now we must work."[20]

While the subtleties and knowledge of the Idiot Typology will be given in subsequent chapters, it is important to remember that the different exercises, techniques and rituals people learn in every school with the aim of spiritual development are merely starting points, and not done for their own sake. Every method is merely an empty casket if it lacks energy, spontaneity and the living power of active work. As a Chinese Zen-Master once said, "It is not important how long you are able to sit. I have observed hens for days sitting on the stick, and they didn't get enlightened." (Who knows what happen with hens...) We have to go further. Basho, the founder of the Zen-inspired Haiku poetry in the 17th century, brought this philosophy to the point: "Don't search for the wisdom of the ancients - look for what they had searched for themselves." We are striving to be human vessels for the manifestation of consciousness - a creative, evolutionary act that connects us to a deeper understanding of the "Creative Intelligence" [21] of life.

This book is based on the ideas of Gurdjieff, though I have taken the freedom to interpret his ideas as I have come to understand them. My expertise has grown out of the practical work with groups over the last three decades, especially through my work with John G. Bennett at his "International Academy for Continuous Learning" in Sherborne, Gloucestershire, England (founded in 1971), in which he encouraged individual study and the taking of one's spiritual evolution into one's own hands. Gurdjieff and Bennett were "stations of transmission" for the conscious force helping human evolution, or "baraka", available to us all. Near the end of his life, in response to a question about whether personal guidance of a pupil through a teacher is still is possible in the modern age, Bennett answered, "No. I don't mean that this personal relationship of a teacher with one pupil is no longer possible, but is no longer *adequate*. The world has grown, and its spiritual needs are so great that this restricted method of transmission is no longer sufficient. Certainly it continues, and will always continue. There is the universal *baraka*. There is the *baraka* of a particular tradition and there is the personal *baraka*..."[22] The universal *baraka* pervades the world and people can become sensitive to it and receive it. Every group or individual working towards spiritual evolution is working towards receiving this *baraka*.

The way of self-determined development is very difficult – comparable to Indiana Jones' perilous travels and quests. Just as he traveled over long foot-bridges over steep divides, clinging desperately to a ropy handrail, so do we travel over the tight-wire of our psychological yearnings, seeking the comfort of proven strategies, ways and groups. However, this can create dependencies, even cult-like or sectarian relationships within or between different groups. Group work is very important, but, as Bennett once said, "There is nothing, not even God, that can give us freedom. Our Loving Creator can do no more than give us the possibility of freedom; our freedom then can be earned. Almost everything else can be given to us, but not freedom."[23] In the end, we are alone, striving idiotically towards idiocy, in both meanings of the word.

Gurdjieff intended that his teaching be transmitted to later generations of committed, determined and seeking people – he named his Magnum Opus: "Beelzebub's tales to his Grandson". We are his grandchildren, inheritors of this teaching. During my work over the last 40 years, I have come to the conclusion that the "Fourth Way" as presented by Gurdjieff doesn't fulfill all the needs of the present day, especially when trapped in dogma or institutional forms. Gurdjieff initiated and transmitted this teaching, but it is an unfinished circle that needs your hand to complete.

If (as I hope) you think about, work to understand, and put into practice, the material presented within these covers, then the meaning of this book can be considered to be fulfilled.

2. "To the Health of All Ordinary Idiots"
– The Ritual Feast

"Every ritual is a manifestation and every kind of shared religious experience involves some kind of ritual."
John G. Bennett

Cooking and eating are transformational processes. This concept is the basis for many religious traditions and rituals, from the Love Feasts of Dionysus to the practice of Communion. Eating together connects people, providing nutrition for both body and spirit. Like the holy cross, we can be connected with the horizontal plane of worldly knowledge and ideas, as well as the vertical plane of timelessness and spacelessness – a mysterious "something higher". In ancient cultures, as well as in some circles today, the belief was held that we are in a cycle of "mutual maintenance" with beings of a higher form. As we eat, so we are eaten. We are given food, and in turn, become food ourselves. The community becomes food for the world above, the heavenly bodies. A ritual meal is seen as an opportunity to embody this exchange, by partaking of food and by offering a sacrifice in the form of spirits, incense, food or meditation, to ensure the continued connection with mankind, the fertility of the women or the fruitfulness of the fields.

Many teachers, from the ancient Greek philosopher's Symposiums to Jesus in the Last Supper, and beyond, have used the opportunity of the ritual feast to transmit knowledge and insights. It was through Gurdjieff's Feast of the Idiots (also known as the Toast of the Idiots), that one could get a direct "taste" of the experience of a School of the Moment. Anthony Blake points out that the ritual meal has a much deeper significance than we generally perceive, and that our role during the meal is to become conscious of the transformation of our bodily foods into the energies that allow us to live. In this way, we connect our lives with life at a higher scale. From the microcosm of our cells' division to the macrocosm of our place in the universe, we connect our lives with the immutable force that exists beyond ourselves.

Gurdjieff adopted the ritual meal as a teaching method from his teachers in the east, bringing it to the west in this particular form. How much he made up or how much is based on the known ritual feasts of the Middle East and the Caucasus is unclear. Elizabeth Bennett, a student of Gurdjieff from 1948-9, took part in many of his "Feasts of the Idiots". She writes, "When he had learned it (I thought he said in Tibet, but I can't be certain), he had decided to make use of it to teach people, though really it was not his to use, and for this the initiate persons did not like him. But in the new world it would be used. Because he is going to make war on the old world: he is going to break our so-called God, with the long beard and the comb in his vest pocket."

Gurdjieff held the ritual meal at least once a day, often twice. During the afternoon before the meals people practiced or performed the Movements in a dance hall. Then they collected with Gurdjieff in his salon in Paris, where he held the meal in the cramped quarters of his flat, at Rue des Colonels Renard No. 6. The sometimes 50 participants had to crowd into a rather small room not bigger than an ordinary living room of a middle class house. The people sat near each other, nobody could really move. Rina Hands recalls, "The salon is half a small drawing room with a china cabinet standing across the closed double doors. This is crammed with dolls and all sorts of rather awful ornaments. Every wall in the room is completely covered with pictures and decorations. Even the curtains drawn across the windows have quantities of brooches and Christmas tree decorations pinned on them. The room itself was packed with people sitting on chairs, stools and the floor."[24]

Before the meal there was often a reading of his work *Beelzebub's Tales to His Grandson*, or sometimes from Ouspensky's *Fragments of an Unknown Teaching* (published as *In Search of the Miraculous*), or some other pertinent writing to set the tone. To concentrate attention on this text was not easy, especially when Gurdjieff was present, as he radiated a kind of inquisitive energy; it was an environment in which one could easily become self-conscious, instead of conscious of oneself. Gurdjieff's band-worm sentences with many unknown and special terms were a great challenge to the intellect. He used language in such a way as to draw you out of your mind (or drive you out of your mind). To fully understand his writings, one must find another way to pay attention, absorbing the writings as though your skin were porous or as though the text were a painting, or any other trick you could make up to get your intellect and conditioning out of the way. A pertinent example from *Beelzebub's Tales to his Grandson*: "And so, my boy, the chief peculiarity of the Omnipresent-Okidanokh, in the given case, is that the process of 'Djartklom' proceeds in it within the presence of every being also but not from being in contact with the emanations of any large cosmic concentration..." and so on.[25] As the process of "Djartklom" brings about the unification of the three forces, the active, receptive, and reconciling forces, into one creative will, so the process of the meal can open up the participant to the direct perception of the various scales of action taking place in and through him.

After the reading he sometimes played his harmonium, which seemed to create a profound emotional impact on his students.[26] Kathryn Hulme writes about one such occasion in December 1936, "The master rewarded us handsomely with gourmet dinners, enthralling table talk, and, above all, with the music he played for us afterwards on his small hand accordion. This was the music of prayer – haunting, disturbing, indescribably beautiful, music calculated to arouse the deepest longings hidden in the heart of man."[27]

After the readings, the participants proceeded from the salon to the very narrow dining room, in which they were obliged to sit very near each other around the table due to the limited space. By the time the last person had taken a seat, people were comically close and no one could move. "This was just the other part of the drawing room", Rina Hands recalls, "There was so much furniture you would think there would scarcely be room for people. A long table filled the centre and there were also two side tables, a sideboard and an upright piano. Mr. Gurdjieff's place occupied about one half of one side of the long table. In front of him was an enormous tray stacked with all sorts of things – bottles, dried meats, sweetmeats and heaven knows what else – and in addition, a huge array of bottles of alcohol was in the middle of the table to his left. Behind this sat a man called the [Verseur] who dispensed the alcohol to everyone for drinking the toasts – men to drink one glass for three toasts, women one glass for six."[28]

Gurdjieff used a special sitting order. On the Director's left sat the man responsible for pouring drinks, the *Verseur*. On the right of Gurdjieff sat *Bouche d'Egout*, the "mouth of the gully", sometimes also called *Egout* or *Poubelle*, meaning "dustbin", whose job it was to eat what Gurdjieff didn't (and in most reported cases, he ate little or nothing). Lastly, the *Egout pour Sweet* had a special function, namely to eat Gurdjieff's pudding or dessert should he not want it.[29]

The meals were served family-style, in big bowls that were passed down through the group. First was served the "Gurdjieff-salad", a hodge-podge of finely cut vegetables, oil and vinegar. No one could eat until Gurdjieff called out the first toast, "To the

28

health of all Ordinary Idiots". If someone had been selected as an Ordinary Idiot - in most cases a child was chosen - the Director added, "and also to your health, so on and so forth." As a general rule, newcomers were made honored guests of the ritual, though he or she could only take part by listening or memorizing the sequence of Idiots. Should the guest come to a second meal, they would have to choose. This he or she communicated to the Director by writing it down on his invitation card, and it is rumored that those in possession of such a card would be welcomed in esoteric communities around the world as initiates of the Science of Idiotism. Said Gurdjieff, "There are monasteries in central Asia where you are immediately admitted."

The salad seemed to be famous in its own right. The niece of Gurdjieff, Luba Gurdjieff, owned a famous Russian restaurant in London until the mid-seventies of the last century and gives us some insight into the salad's making, "… We had something like it lots of times - not for big occasions, but when somebody was coming, somebody new to impress, you know, my uncle would say in a big whisper, 'That is my salad'. He used to come into the kitchen sometimes and make it himself. He tasted all the time. Valya and I and my auntie used to cut, cut, cut, and give it to him.... Then he says, 'that's enough cut. You good girl. Make a big bowl like that'."[30] She goes on, "And you can't have a recipe for it. It costs the earth! You put anything you can find in that thing: chopped tomatoes, cucumbers, radishes, celery, any vegetable you can find - only raw vegetables. No lettuce, because lettuce gets very soft. It used to have nuts in it; it used to have green olives you cut in pieces away from the stone; it used to have sometimes prunes in small pieces - it was like a dustbin. Chutney - he used to put lots of chutney. And he used to like those little green things in vinegar - capers. Twenty, thirty things used to go in that salad. Sometimes he would even put apples - any kind of apples. I think he would put anything he could find in there...

And dressing: he just put on a little bit of vinegar and then some oil. You never do anything to it; just chew it."[31] The beauty of the salad is – not only that it tastes excellent – but also that it is such a concise and solid metaphor for this Work, or for any School of the Moment. Use what you can find, don't hold back, and chew, chew, chew!

Soup came after the salad, often a Russian borscht soup, consisting of beets in a bullion base and a dollop of cream. Luba offers the recipe in her book.[32] But it also was surprising. Rina Hands remembers that it was delicious, "but, alas, stone-cold". The main course was meat, brown rice and vegetables, often cabbage. On the table were oriental sweets of all kinds and people smoked a lot so that the room was not only filled with the smell of the food but also with the smoke.

The toasts generally did not proceed past the Twelfth Idiot, due to the fact that so few people have reached a level beyond this point. Gurdjieff told stories relating the characterizations of the Idiots, inviting and challenging the ensuing discussion. "When the toast to all Compassionate Idiots was given, he suddenly looked right down the table to me and asked, 'You Blonde there – natural or not I never know – are you Compassionate Idiot?' I was amazed that he should suggest that there was a grain of compassion in me and I said, 'Oh no, I don't think so.' To this he replied, 'I only ask, excuse.'"[33]

These few impressions demonstrate the formality and the quite specific outer form this ritual took. However within this outer form, the emotional tone and opportunities varied wildly, dependent on the mood of the meal and, of course, the moment. Gurdjieff kept the spirit alive with conflict, jokes, secrets and stories, eliciting curiosity, confusion, and plenty of opportunity for observation. The meal went on until midnight. Nobody really got drunk, but all were very tired in the end. Most probably this was another reason the Feast seldom proceeded beyond Idiot number 12.

Alcohol played an integral role in the ritual feasts of Gurdjieff. Anthony Blake points out in his book *The Intelligent Enneagram* that much of the experience of the feasts may happen less through the discussion, but more through the experience itself, heightened by the intake of certain psychoactive substances. "The intake of certain substances plays an important role, which has a pronounced effect on the human psyche. In Gurdjieff's case, this is the use of alcohol. In other cases it is the food itself, which is transformed into a powerful substance by means of the ritual."[34]

Kenneth Walker explains, "You see, he's a Russian, and Russians always drink a lot of vodka. But there is another and far more important reason why all of G.'s guests have to drink, whatever their private tastes happens to be. A great many people are passing through his hands and he is compelled *to see* them as quickly as possible."[35] Alcohol is able to open up people and sometimes we see hidden traits. But in fact the use of vodka in a ritual can lead to a higher awareness instead of make you drunken, that's my experience.

Not knowing the full dangers of smoking, tobacco was also used, reminiscent of its extensive use in shamanic rituals. During shamanic rituals, the wife of the shaman stands behind him, warding off "bad spirits" with the smoke (though of course, these people smoke natural jungle tobacco not the industrialized poison from Virginia). In honor of this tradition, I still encourage smoking during the ritual (natural tobacco without any additives, of course, or try to get Peruvian *mapacho*).

The "Science of Idiots" was presented in the intensive and dynamic setting of a meal because, through the enhanced attention and perceptions that this sort of ritual evokes, we can more fully grasp or intuit what sort of idiot one is - **who we are**. If the ritual is performed with the right inner attitude, we can get a "taste" of it. Not being able to partake of these meals with Gurdjieff now, but with the hope of recreating it in his spirit, we must create a new setting to evoke the same intensity and result without blindly imitating his forms. After long pondering, I came to the conclusion that it ought to be preserved for the future, though not in a stagnant, formulaic sense, but rather in a dynamic, creative and experiential way. Gurdjieff experimented with his exercises and his teachings, and my own teacher, Mr. Bennett, did the same. Critically important to any teaching is that it doesn't get lost in translation – that while the vessel may differ, the wine remains the same. We need to adapt the teachings to the circumstances of the world and our lives, while preserving the integrity of the core ideas. Therefore, my goal is to present the original teachings of the "Science of the Idiots" as faithfully as possible, while proposing new ideas of how to incorporate it into contemporary life. *This is crucial: that everything that helps us to evolve dynamically on our individual path can and must be of use.*

"We only see what we know", says my artist wife, Nana Nauwald.[36] If one can see it, one <u>is</u> it (a very helpful idea when negatively judging others). Gurdjieff said, "Psychology should be an art, it never can be a science". The understanding of the Idiots is just that – inner knowledge. But we humans are works of art, and the developed faculties of awareness and attention, acquired through study, are mandatory skills to see ourselves properly. Use the tool of the Feast of the Idiots as a structure to walk around, look upon, prod, examine and discuss your own psychology. In chapter 5, I will give the basic procedure - a menu if you will - around which you can piece together a Feast, adding of course, your own "daily specials".

"It is true that the higher worlds are freer, but there is something beyond all this: that each one of us has his or her own perfection. Perfection is perfection; there is no beyond in it. Whoever attains what he is destined for has achieved his perfection and anything else has no meaning. The Work that we hope to enter into is to bring us to our perfection."[37] The "Science of Idiotism" is only meaningful for those who are ready to work at their inner perfection. At the entrance to this "Otherworld" there is written – as the German author Hermann Hesse puts it in his novel, "Steppenwolf":

"Magical Theatre - Admission only for Madmen."

So, if you aren't an Idiot or Madman – or wish to be, please close the book.

3. "Remember Yourself"
Gurdjieff's Transpersonal Psychology

"Remember you come here having already understood the necessity of struggling with yourself - only with yourself. Therefore thank everyone who gives you the opportunity."
G.I. Gurdjieff[38]

"His understanding of the human psyche was such that when he gave a person his special 'idiot' it seemed almost miraculous, for to others it gave a clue to the pattern of the person's behavior; though it took the person sometimes a very long time to see it for himself. Gurdjieff said that the science of idiotism was a mirror in which a man could see himself. Not everyone had the right to be included in a category, of which there were twenty-one. Apart from the toasts, during the day's work he might call a person idiot, *doorak,* in the opposite sense, meaning that he was senseless."[39]

With the notable exception of J. G. Bennett, none of Gurdjieff's pupils worked with the teaching of the Idiots after his death. This was due to the fact that his students were so impressed by the mastery of Gurdjieff's skills, his unique capacity to see beyond the superficial, that there was doubt as to the ritual's effectiveness in any other hands. In fact, "[the] Toast of the Idiots was discontinued immediately on Gurdjieff's death in 1949, it being felt, without his decisive presence, it stood in danger of becoming a mere form without content."[40] However, if it is a science, it does have general features that can be transcribed and interpreted for further experimentation.

Helen Palmer wrote, "Probably Gurdjieff was convinced, that the people of his time were not prepared enough to identify their inner pattern correctly. Although his pupils have worked with the practice of self-observation, Freud's theory of the unconscious was not grounded in Europe, and the pupils didn't have the knowledge of the psychological context, which today we take for granted."[41] For this reason, and perhaps many others, many of Gurdjieff's pupils kept to rigid form after his death, transmitting his ideas completely unchanged. In many so-called "Gurdjieff groups", the general advancements of modern psychology are ignored, creating an ironic orthodoxy on an inherently adaptable system. Only a few of his subsequent followers have made flexibility and experimentation a primary value in their work groups. The aim is the "harmonious development of man" and the holistic growth of the totality of the human being, both the inner (more real) and outer (less real) parts. And from this balance can grow increased consciousness of one's totality. This idea of a "transpersonal psychology" is summed up as follows: The personal and the transpersonal dimensions are different but not separated. Both are part of human experience. Usually a human being has the tendency to concentrate more on one dimension, to experience it as more real, more important. This tendency to prefer one dimension is mirrored in the different views of growth in our own culture. The western view values a man with a strong personality highest - people who are full of activities and who are skilled and clever in the practical aspects of life, who perform efficiently and who fulfill all tasks set before them. The eastern view values a man highest who cultivates his inner, spiritual life. But to realize our whole potential we must include both: the personal and the transpersonal dimension.[42]

Today's psychologists appropriately encourage a well-established and -developed personality, or character.[43] However, the common personality, the "mask", consists of acquired features of humans, forming an outer layer of our being. It is this part of us that is asleep, and is identified with the external world, with political views, fashionable trends and many other social forms of behavior – creating false ideas and illusions about ourselves and the surrounding world. It is like clothing, necessary to live in the world, to keep one warm, comfortable, and socialized. But, it is not one's own; it is a product of imitation – all external impress-sions, sensations, words, movements and feelings have formed themselves on the clay of you.

From the point of view of western psychology, Gurdjieff's ideas are revolutionary, turning traditional frames of reference and value systems on their heads. At the core of this teaching is the idea that humans, by reason of an unconscious process of mechanical reactions and developments, are literally asleep, and as such cannot perceive objective reality. Most probably this unconscious process starts with the self-restriction of the will, i.e. with the entry into the space-time dimension of the material world.[44] At the time of conception, the unborn soul is pure will to live. At birth, the essence is planted, with an individual will, in the being of the child. This essence is the "spiritual being" of the child, that which can mature into a unique individual. The material part of the child's essence is the personality, and includes inherited traits, talents and characteristics. During socialization and education, the child necessarily must form such a protective layer, a mask or shell, made of imitated and learned patterns and habits, around the undeveloped essence. This is called the *personality*. Thinking ourselves fully conscious beings, we take our actions, reactions and habits for granted. We leave ourselves, our surroundings, even time and space, unexamined, thinking only the mask is real.

It is the goal of this work to make ourselves more conscious – to see these patterns of the personality, and to unburden, integrate and develop that which is more real inside of us: our Essence. Gurdjieff called the technique to accomplish this "self-remembering", putting the parts together. If you are in the state of self-remembering you are awake, i.e. really conscious, with all centers synchronized.

Gurdjieff's psychology can be understood in this way: that self-realization involves the recognition and balance of the internal and external worlds, and the continual pursuit of internal refinement. Only through work on ourselves are we able to escape the misery and burdens of this level of existence, and find meaning and fulfillment with the Will of creation, which lies beyond our typical illusions of the world.

I see these ideas as wonderfully practical in my own quest for experience and insight. Those of us who occupy ourselves with these ideas more than sixty years after Gurdjieff's death cannot take them for granted, cannot take them as dogmatic or complete. In fact, quite the opposite, we must rigorously examine and re-examine these ideas and our efforts to understand them. His psychology is really a combination of art and science as he said himself -, and it begs us to respond accordingly.

Gurdjieff used different and changing concepts to explain his psychology. One approach we find in the report of his teaching written down by P. D. Ouspensky with the title *In Search of the Miraculous*. Here he says, "Essence is the truth in man; personality is the false. ... As a rule a man's essence is either primitive, savage, and childish, or else simply stupid. The development of essence depends on work on oneself."[45] In a later talk, in 1924, he says, "Essence is I - it is our heredity, type, character, nature. Personality is an accidental thing - upbringing, education, and points of view - everything external. It is like the clothes you wear, your artificial mask, the result of your upbringing, of the influence of your surroundings, opinions..."[46] In the former teaching he also says, "A man's Real I, his individuality, can grow only from his essence. It can be said that a man's individuality is his essence, grown up, mature."[47]

This is very important in view of the "Science of Idiots". With work on ourselves the essence can grow, and we step up the "ladder of reason" as Gurdjieff calls the different stages of the idiots.

I will make this point clearer: *Personality*, having been created through multiple influences, is multi-fold and so humans have many "I's". This means that it speaks and acts from many different places, none of which is based in our own individuality, but all of which take the mantle and claim dominion while in control. This creates the internal situation wrought with conflicts and hypocrisies with which we are all familiar. For example: one part of the personality - one "I" - says "I would like to lose weight! I shall eat only grapefruit in the morning and do without butter on my toast!" However, by the time morning comes around, quite a different "I" is in control and, if it remembers at all, quite probably will dismiss the idea and go about its normal routine, eating whatever is habitual and maybe the leftovers as well. More importantly, one may hope to not be negative. But, as we have no center, no permanent controller of things, no Master, no "Real I", our efforts are thwarted by ourselves as soon as the attention and intention are gone, and often even earlier.

While the essence is the core of our real being, our individuality, personality corresponds to the outer layer of our being, working mainly with "automatic" and "sensitive" energies,[48] and therefore it is not really "conscious". Bennett makes this distinction with the terms "material essence" and "spiritual essence". He says, "The body comes almost entirely by heredity… The soul is made out of the material of the selfhood. The part with which we are born is mainly… in the divided self, that is, our character.[49] This can be called 'the material essence' because it is a pattern of energies. … The spirit … means for me the same as 'spiritual essence'. It is a pattern of qualities that is not in any way material, and therefore it is not subject to the conditions of time and place."[50]

The term "personality" very often is used synonymously with "character", but in my understanding personality is much more the socialized side of humans, while the real character, the material essence, is an individual pattern similar to our fingerprints, and is the functional aspect of the spiritual essence. While the latter is not bound by time and space, personality develops within time and space and responds to the needs of the body in the physical world. "Perhaps the most important idea to help us understand the idea of the spiritual essence is the realization that our destiny is not determined by our character [material essence], but by our *spiritual qualities* [spiritual essence]."[51] The material side of our being acts in the world and the spiritual side has the potential to evolve into our unique individuality.

The idea of our two-fold nature (the material and spiritual essences) is reflected in the ideas of quantum physics with the idea that matter and energy are only different forms of the same phenomenon – particle and wave. Matter is a form of energy that can be made visible or materialized or can be made un-materialized and invisible. It is similar with humans... The quantum physicist Amit Goswami states, "The spectrum of self-consciousness consists of states of forms, with which the consciousness identifies during the different steps of evolution of human beings. At the lower end the whole spectrum is embraced by the personal unconscious, at the upper stage by the collective unconscious. However, every stage is in consciousness. The scheme should not be understood hierarchically, but as something which develops or grows. The higher we develop, the more we lose our ego until on the highest level there doesn't exist a distinguishable identity with the ego."[52]

We can observe our character through un-critical observation of things we are good at – natural talents and tendencies that may

40

exhibit themselves in areas of craft or surgery or in accuracy of expression in writing or painting, for example. We also may find this true personality manifesting itself in its ability to fulfill basic obligations, such as taking out the garbage every Monday without fail, or in having unwavering feelings for other people, or by being able to bear difficulties and conflicts without inappropriate or undue emotional overlay. This is the part of ourselves that can find value and make uncelebrated efforts. But character traits also consist of emotions and actions. Therefore there can be a "good" or a "bad" character. What Gurdjieff is up to in his "Science of Idiotism" is to show special character traits which come up as we work on ourselves. But they are not static and therefore we can climb up the ladder to becoming more integrated beings.

The "false" personality, in contrast, makes only efforts that reward itself, but has many illusions about itself that would indicate otherwise. The behavior of our personality is primarily acquired through socialization during childhood. It is by definition imbalanced and consists of fears, over-sensitivities, jealousies, anger, etc., that are imprinted quite early. As we grow, we imitate the behaviors that allow us to function in our society – more emphasis is placed on external qualities than internal. We must function, earn money, support a family, and so on. Through our personality in general, we interact in the world, developing feelings of control and authority over our material world and ourselves. Being full of imprinted habits, justifications and attitudes, the personality is not really helpful to anything but the perpetuation of itself. These attitudes, which primarily rotate around the two giants Pride and Vanity, become wired into our brains, and so we cannot perceive reality correctly.

"It is not so easy to see what the divided self [our character] is about. It is far deeper than the level of reaction. For the greater parts of our lives, the divided self may be no more than a pattern that accompanies us from birth and limits the kinds of relationships that we can form. We can only get at it indirectly, by finding out, for example, what we 'cannot do' in situations, such as take the initiative or keep to a plan and so on, which gives us a clue to our type. The observation of our typical behaviors can lead us to understand that there is 'something' in us which is imposing a pattern of what is possible and impossible for us to do, that is not due to external conditioning or the state of our mechanism [i.e. our personality]. Type is rather like a style of life that has almost infinite possibilities of variation. But we must remember that we are rather like actors who have a very limited repertoire of roles. It is almost impossible to make ourselves act in a way that is not typical."[53]

Gerald Hüther, a professor of neurophysiology in Göttingen, Germany, describes the patterns and habits that develop in our brain in terms of modern neurology. He states that people's brains are composed of certain patterns of highly complex "wired" nerve cells and that these patterns are laid down by early experience, which continues to instruct the pattern of our experience through life. Our thinking, feelings and actions, in fact all of our reactions are based upon the wiring of these circuits. When a certain circuit is activated by a particular experience, it reacts mechanically, stimulating a pre-determined response[54].

We consist of a multitude of ideas and personas, each of which take the mantle and assume our identity. "Today you are convinced of one thing - you believe it and want it. Tomorrow, under another influence, your beliefs, your desires become different. All the material constituting your personality may be completely changed artificially or accidentally with a change in your surrounding conditions and place - and this in a very short time."[55]

A most dangerous illusion that we share is the illusion that we can DO, that we are not asleep, that our everyday existence is based on conscious efforts and decisions. If we think we are conscious, then all striving stops. Why seek what one already has? The danger here lays in our identification with ourselves, with what we think we can do and that we think our reactions are interesting. It is tricky because the personality can function (to a better or worse degree) within the material world, however it cannot function intentionally. Ironically, because it thinks it can. Unquestioningly, we believe these illusions of ourselves: that we are pretty, handsome, generous, kind, right, conscious – and use these attitudes as justifications for all sorts of atrocious behavior. While maintaining the skills acquired through life, we must learn to see this identification and separate from it, let loose its hold, because when the personality is strengthened, the essence remains weak. Our goal, then, physiologically speaking, is nothing less than the actual rewiring of our brains; stopping the habitual reactions and allowing for new synapses to be activated, and allowing for spontaneous, non-mechanical and genuine responses to our environment.

It is a skill to learn to study and observe oneself impartially, but it is this impartiality that allows one to separate from the actions and identities of the personality. After sufficient time and effort, one can begin to integrate what one has learned about one's personality into a larger picture of the whole. The already mentioned teaching of "psycho-synthesis" emphasizes the importance of this holistic integration.[56] The central concern of most kinds of psychotherapy is the dealing with deficiencies in specific personality functions or with the conflicts between them. The best point of departure to personal self-realization aims at the positive development of special aspects of the essence and helps with the gradual integration into a dynamic whole. Also the insight grows that personal self realization not only consists of the harmonization of all aspects of the character, but also in the gradual emergence and strengthening of the "I", the center of the personal identity. The integrated essence slowly builds itself around the real "I".

Gurdjieff demonstrated the separation between the internal and external manifestations of people in an experiment of which Ouspensky reports. Gurdjieff announced that he wanted to carry out an experiment on the separation of personality from essence. The method was not described by Ouspensky but I think he did use Hashish and not alcohol, which at this time in Russia was not illegal. The two persons involved in this experiment had been a younger man with a prominent position, who played a kind of fool, and an older man, who wasn't taken serious because he talked too much. Some time after the intake of the substance Gurdjieff gave a hint to the other participants to observe. The talkative person suddenly became silent and had a different voice and told some observation about himself in a clear, simple, and intelligible manner without superfluous words. "The younger one began to listen to the talk and then spoke. All of us looked at one another. His voice had become different." The conversation went on and after a while the elder spoke "in such a serious voice and with such serious intonations that we all looked at one another: '*I think I should like some raspberry jam.*"[57] This experiment showed clearly to the people present that in many cases very little remains of a person's usual opinions, fears and so on, when the personality was put to sleep.

The experiment also shows that we very often take the appearance of a personality, its "originality" or place in society, for its special individuality, but, as Gurdjieff states, "a very important moment in the work on oneself is when a man begins to distinguish between his personality and his essence. A man's Real I, his individuality, can grow only from his essence. It can be said that a man's individuality is his essence, grown up, mature. But in order to enable essence to grow up, it is first of all necessary to weaken the constant pressure of personality upon it, because the obstacles to the growth of essence are contained in personality."[58]

A good functioning personality is not only a shield against the outer world, but also necessary to survival in our society. Psychological work based on Gurdjieff's teaching shouldn't devalue the personality, rather it should strive to develop both parts - personality and essence - until the core of the essence can take control and guide the personality, not the other way around.

Chief Feature or Chief Weakness

"We only are able to see our chief feature when we are able to bear it."
Maurice Nicoll

I hope I have made it clear by now why Gurdjieff emphasized a "holistic" and "synchronized" development of man - the integration of all sides of a person. By seeing, accepting and integrating all sides of ourselves, from talent to fault, we bring ourselves from the darkness of self-delusion into the light of consciousness. Without harmonized functions and the development of the essence we cannot bring forth our Real I, our real identity. And if we haven't found our real identity we cannot be ourselves and consequently not an "Idiot". The idea that we cannot, in our present state, see ourselves is a generally accepted idea by today's psychologists. If we want to live a fuller life and reach our potential, we have to discover our blind spots, our defense mechanisms. Unconscious defenses, which are called "buffers" by Gurdjieff, distort our perception of reality.

We all have favorite buffers; first lines of defense that help ensure the longevity of our favorite illusions, which prevent us from experiencing reality. However, each of us has a particular tendency, a chief weakness, called in this system "Chief Feature", which acts as the central axis around which our personal life rotates. It is so close to us that we don't see it – don't recognize how it colors every decision and interaction. It is our rose-colored glasses. Everybody has such a central character trait. "If by means of work over a long period a man begins to awaken to himself, he is going in the direction of awakening to his Chief Feature... All the work that we do at present is connected with awakening to ourselves, with becoming more aware of ourselves, with letting light in to ourselves. Consciousness is light. If you begin to observe yourself uncritically you let in light. Eventually this light will show up Chief Feature but not until you have caught hold of the rope, of something to hold you... I advise you all not to identify with the words Chief Feature. Try simply to understand that everything, all your reactions, your attitudes, your behavior, your thoughts and feelings revolve round a central axle, which keeps them fixed. If one can see one of these spokes, it is like taking a photograph. Then one sees another spoke, and so on. They all lead to the same thing in the centre."[59]

David Kherdian struggled for a long time to find his Chief Feature, a process of learning to separate from oneself to develop the capacity to see oneself more objectively (to take the glasses off, if only for a moment). "I had begun to think I would never discover my Chief Feature. From everything I had read, it seemed to be the crux of the teaching, the ultimate lever on which everything rose and fell. In the beginning, I had thought that if I found my Chief Feature my major problem would be solved, although how I had imagined my problems would be solved by this revelation I could no longer remember. Mrs. Staveley[60] agreed with me that my Chief Feature was probably grounded in self love, but of course that was too general to have any meaning. One had to know what it was *exactly* because it was said to manifest always, in everything, and therefore determine each and every outcome of one's life.

46

"And then, on one of our special trips to Portland, where the three of us sometimes went for lunch, she told me what my Chief Feature was: *Complaining.*

"Complaining?" I muttered. "Complaining!" Isn't that amazing, I thought to myself, the one thing I have *never* done. I gave her a puzzled look, but made no comment.... I asked myself how something that was so clear to everyone else could be so opaque for me. And so hidden.... Finally, it dawned on me. What others called complaining, I was calling something else. But, ironically, I had no name for it. What I was probably doing, or thought I was doing, was *correcting the situation.*"[61]

Our Chief Feature is the "blind spot" in our character and obstructs our way to self-development because it is our primary self-delusion. It is an expression of a pattern of basic desires, wishes or motives, reacting mechanically and always in the same way to people or situations. The Chief Feature lies deeply hidden in our feelings and distorts our view of reality.

"Those around him see a man's chief feature however hidden it may be. Of course they cannot always define it. But their definitions are often very good and very near. Take nicknames. Nicknames sometimes define chief features very well."[62] Ask someone close to you how he or she would evaluate or characterize you. Naïve? Pompous? Cowardly? Excitable? Contrary? What are your goals? What gets in your way? What is your excuse? How do you justify your excuse? These are all clues.

The Chief Feature is difficult to see, because it is so underlying to the entire personality, creating the very foundation of our attitudes, preferences and justifications. This is critical because through self-observation you can learn, in the words of Maurice Nicoll "to bear the chief feature". And if you can bear it, then you are on your way to knowing it, and if you know it, you can learn to use it.

P. D. Ouspensky says that we should find our Chief Feature by ourselves. Only when one really *feels* it will one know that it's real. Until we can emotionally and deeply understand how our chief feature negatively impacts our lives and interactions, how it controls us and keeps us from our goals, we will "buffer" it and forget it. It is like a wound, an area that is inflexible and causes us to not be able to adapt to situations, but rather to always react in the same way. It is a distorted pattern of response springing mechanically from deep within. "In no case can anyone be told his or her Chief Feature because no one would believe it and then no one could stand it. The action of the Work gradually brings an individual to the point of glimpsing of it. It is like being undermined: it is incredible: it is like being accused of theft or murder..."[63]

Jane Heap, a student of Gurdjieff, gives an important hint as to how we can learn about our chief feature: "In looking for your Chief Feature, don't follow type and don't follow whim... The range is so small – basically based on five things - five interests control our actions - *Greed - Self-Pride - Lying - Fear - Sex*. Chief Feature is one or a combination of these. Take your long list and reduce it to this. Find it. It is a short-cut to consciousness. Once found, use it consciously."[64]

But interestingly, Chief Feature also carries with it a clue, because it is a skewed reaction of one's real character. If you can observe it long enough, get to know this strange beast that takes your name and acts in your stead in the world, you can begin to see what it may look like when the quality behind it comes forward. In other words, you begin to have a clue as to your true identity, a key to your essence. There is a reason that you have a different chief feature than I do. While everyone's chief feature is based on basically the same few things, mentioned in Heap's quotation above, what lays underneath it is a unique quality that has adjusted poorly to everyday life; a very distorted reflection of something deep and true within our essence. The goal then isn't to be rid of the Chief Feature, but rather to *know* it and be its master so that it isn't whipping you around, controlling all decisions and living your life. As Gurdjieff says, it is an *involuntary manifestation*. If we can transform this wound to strength, we can live in our real character; we can live according to our talents.

"Chief Feature in each one of us is a key to our actions and manifestations. It tips the scales. Always the same motive moves Chief Feature. It is like the bias in bowling, which prevents the ball going straight. Always Chief Feature makes us go off at a tangent. It is something mechanical and imaginary and is found in the emotional part of essence. It gives the tone pitch to the three centers and forms the pattern of our wishes. It arises from one or more of the seven deadly sins, but chiefly from self-love and vanity. One can discover it by becoming more conscious; and its discovery brings an increase in consciousness", explained C. S. Nott, who studied extensively with Gurdjieff.[65]

When you have worked to this extent on yourself you can understand that the Chief Feature is a blind spot of the character, while the "Idiot" is of the real being. Chief Feature prevents us from gaining contact to what is most real within us, from becoming an Idiot, because it is a mechanical reaction of the personality. On the other hand, if it is made conscious, it can become a defining strength. For example, David Kherdian's Chief Feature of "complaining" becomes a strength when he learns instead to *see the real order of things*. The weakness can be turned into a "sword", a great strength.

The being is not fixed, it can grow and unfold with time, and therefore if you step up "the ladder of reason", as Gurdjieff called it, you can become what you really are. This also is the difference between doing and being: you *do* according to your will type[66] and you *are* according to your inner essence. Your being manifests through your character: you can only *do* what you *are*.

Through difficult events, intentional efforts, grace, or even luck, we are occasionally awakened to moments of "something higher", a brief glimpse of relative freedom from personality. We work on ourselves to experience longer, deeper and more intentional periods of this freedom. This work on ourselves can allow us to become more conscious of our habitual reactions, and then, through long work on ourselves, break free of some of our mechanical intellectual, emotional and physical/sensory routines. However, the wish to enhance consciousness, to loosen the grip of our mechanical selves, to actually unwind the patterns of our neurons, requires tremendous perseverance. Arguably, this perseverance can only come with the re-aligning of ourselves, and of our priorities. Here, we begin to turn "right-side-up". When we are sufficiently dissatisfied with our mechanical reactions and when we have become disillusioned with the glittering gold of the imagined, then room is made within ourselves to experience something quite different: reality.

4. The Science of Idiotism

"If you are looking for enlightenment, look into the human face. In its laughter you will find the essence of the ultimate truth."
Jelaluddin Rumi

Gurdjieff's idiot typology characterizes the inner development of being until we arrive at the core of our essence. As long as personality is still active, and is playing out its habitual, static roles, we are trapped within our fixations such as pride, jealousy and greed, and the mechanical reactions arising from Chief Feature. But if we embrace the qualities of our innermost being, giving reign to higher parts within ourselves, it is possible to ascend the ladder of reason and discover our real task and role in life. The origin of the "Science of Idiots" was most likely also associated with a desire to illustrate the individual connection of people to the Work – or any spiritual Path. One finds the outlined types everywhere, in some version or other. René Zuber explains, "The complete construction of the hierarchy of the idiots has been probably only an astonishing design, which should help us to discover in other people and in ourselves certain deep impregnated peculiarities, which we couldn't see without this structure of the idiots. It is a game of reflections - during its procedure the other people helped us to see our own picture."[67]

Since our self-knowledge has not grown far enough to understand our real predicament, we ought initially to take on the Idiot that seems intuitively closest to what we perceive ourselves to be. Gurdjieff spoke often of the necessity to "act" a role in life without identifying oneself with it. Be *in* life, but not *of* it. A hint of this attitude is given by Elizabeth Bennett, "He (Gurdjieff) scolded one of Miss Heap's group for not having chosen an Idiot, after being here six days, and the girl said she didn't know which to choose - always she wanted to choose a different one. He did not like this, and said this was 'dishonest' in her, and such uncertainty was a sure sign 'that you are not honest'."[68] Gurdjieff's students were expected to continually and vigilantly strive to discover their own idiocy. At every level of development, there is a death and a resurrection – called in Sufism *fana* and *baqa* - before one reaches a new level of reason. "Therefore", as Bennett hints to us, "every time we remember ourselves, this is evidence that going up is possible."

Like different colors of a rainbow, each Idiot is a part of our identity. Every one of us has the essential qualities of each Idiot, of complacency, of compassion, of hopelessness, of squirming, and so forth. In the same way that G. studied men as "machines", as having three brains, and presented this knowledge to us for further study, so we should look deeper, and see how these ideas can be incorporated into our daily lives. At this point in time, we know much more about the psychology and the physiology of the brain; we know how the acts of perception and attention function, requiring direct involvement of the brain. We even know that these mechanisms cannot be isolated from the brain, even though "consciousness" is a field independent of the brain. Gurdjieff explained, "We are supposed to be seeking for reality here, so we should all be idiots: but no one can <u>make</u> you an idiot. You must choose it for yourself. That is why everyone who visits us here and wishes to remain in contact with us, is allowed to choose his own idiot. Then all the rest of us will wish from our hearts that he will truly become that idiot."[69]

With his "Science of the Idiots", Gurdjieff has given a clue to the essential behavioral structures that people develop as they work on themselves on a path to self-realization. His descriptions were tailored to the special circumstances of the ritual meals, as well as the special work conditions in his presence. I suppose that alcohol and humor gave an additional spice to further the understanding of his mostly cryptic formulations, which are, indeed, "works of art". The Idiots have something archetypal about them; they are elaborate paintings of a whole complex of characteristics and behavioral patterns that can be seen in everyone.

In our everyday observation of people, we certainly see people who act and behave in very typical ways. If a certain typical situation arises, one knows that he or she will react in a certain way. The spurned housewife will express outrage at her husband's inattention, but will respond with tearful forgiveness when he drops to one knee, proclaiming (and believing) "things will change". These situations play out as though they were written out beforehand, and in a sense they are, because these are mechanical reactions created by culture and imitation. Another example, taken from the Idiot Typology, is how the "Compassionate Idiot" (complete explanations of the Idiots follow shortly) will always take a stand for animal or human rights, even when considerable risk is involved. However, if the person is acting from a sense of personal ambition or glory then the raw, objective action is polluted by the personality, and only the ego is fed. In Gurdjieff's words, this person then becomes "antipathetic". The goal then, is to embody typical "compassionate" action, without identification, and from a sense of exploration and play. Can you do that?

A "Hopeless Idiot" will entangle himself in activities that are deviations to his aims. If he deviates from a sense of greed, (i.e.: wanting all possible information on all possible subjects for the benefit and enlightenment of himself) then this Idiot will not undo his knot. What if he deviates out of innocence? Then, he has hope.

A "Squirming Idiot" always asks his friends for advice, but promptly ignores it. If he ignores the advice-giver from a sense of vanity, from a sense of already knowing, he cannot be helped. Have you not observed such behavior amongst your friends?

Yourself? The only problem with behaving in these ways is that we forget that there is a difference between these behaviors and ourselves. When we don't consciously perceive this important difference, we become stuck, fixated, and so cannot change and are not free.

How people react to other people and their environment says a lot about them. The "Idiots" point out typical reactions to essential challenges. For example, if we detect certain behavior in a certain person, chances are this behavior will rear itself often. The Idiot who doesn't accept help or advice will call us early in the morning, complaining about a problem. We listen patiently to the problem (if we are "Compassionate"), which is eerily similar to last week's upset, and we offer advice, only to hear that it has been ignored again (often to his/her disadvantage). And the pattern repeats.

As we know from brain research, we experience the world through perceived "virtual realities"; more than 95% of our perception is constructed in our heads. We are therefore unable to see the whole picture, we only see aspects of the reality and the rest is put together unconsciously by the work of the neurons in the brain. The "Science of the Idiots" shows us different aspects of the essential behavioral patterns of humans. Like prismatic reflections, they are not fixed, but rather colors of the whole spectrum. During our lives, especially if we "work on ourselves" to develop our essence, we move through the different characteristics, which then have hold of us at different times and with different intensities. In the descriptions of the Idiots you will find a "positive" and a "negative" aspect. These are hints to the expressions either of outer or the inner part of the "divided self".

During the ritual meals, only the first twelve Idiots would be toasted, not only due to fatigue, but also because these first idiots represent the most common behaviors in everyday life and in relationships. The first nine Idiots generally represent patterns of the "material essence", or character, but nevertheless express something essential. For instance, the "Super Idiot" imagines that he is "something special" because he started on a spiritual path. But this fantasy he has of himself obscures the fact that he is, indeed, special; that his essence is unique and has undiscovered qualities that define his individuality. Without directed observation of and work on ourselves, we are prone to getting stuck in one or other peculiarity. When, however, we are able to experience our real being, we are able to see this "false" personality, and are able to put it aside. With increased self-knowledge, we are able to weaken it and bring out another weakness, habit, identification. Then we move up the "ladder of reason", as the hierarchy of Idiots is sometimes called, and experience another variation of human peculiarities.

At this point you could assert that the descriptions of the idiot types are similar to astrological classifications. For example, a Libra always strives for justice or tries to create harmony within a group. A Capricorn will always have problems opening her/himself to other people, often introverted and brooding. An Aquarius will always try to see things relatively, from several perspectives. We could also draw parallels to a planetary type classification: A Mars type will always fight for something, if it concerns himself. A Venus type will tend to see the beauty of everything, and a Jupiter type always finds ways to be successful. I only want to show the difference between these typologies: principally, that astrological and planetary typologies show basic features of an essence type – that which doesn't change over the course of a lifetime. The Idiot Typology, in contrast, illustrates human patterns of behavior and reaction and, as such, can be navigated. Another important detail: If someone were able to overcome the particular compulsive behavior of their Idiot, that person would subsequently have the ability to manifest the act of that Idiot, have power over the manifestation of that behavior. For example, to pass beyond the Compassionate Idiot doesn't mean that one loses the ability to be compassionate, but can now act compassionately (or not) from choice instead of compulsion. The Idiots are therefore like a training ground, illustrating how archetypal behaviors can be either strengths or weaknesses, depending on who's in charge – it or you.

With the insight and the experience of knowing and understanding your type of Idiot, and after overcoming the associated patterns of behavior and through stepping up the ladder of reason, we reach the core of this psychology. We learn to see our automatic patterns, and that this "seeing", this realization, is a form of deep enlightenment that affects our entire being. Only through seeing these automatic and reactive patterns can we overcome them. If we have observed and overcome several of these behaviors, we are able to begin to break loose from other previously unconscious patterns. Like a ripple in water, efforts on oneself have broad effect. For example, if a "Hopeless Idiot" attains a certain level of self-consciousness and develops the will to really work on himself, instead of just reading about it, he will be free to endure the inner conflict between the hope to achieve something and the realization of it. Then he can act differently and is able to "jump over his own shadow". This type of freedom is the goal of the Science of the Idiots.

Gurdjieff practiced the ritual meal every day for many years. Many of his pupils took part for months - even years - although the process of the ritual with its food, toasts and descriptions remained essentially the same. This may seem a strange training method. But as with any training or exercise that one does with any regularity, the main thing is to learn by doing – in this case, to work with others in the objective study of the rainbow of one's reactions, with the further goal of increased consciousness.

With the ritual dances, the Movements, we reach one part of awareness. These exercises work through the 'moving apparatus', helping to overcome fixed physical, emotional or intellectual patterns and integrate all centers or brains. But psychological patterns, the deeper emotions and essential qualities – with exceptions - are not very much affected by this kind of exercise. In many cases, people learn to control their bodily performance and learn to know some of their reactions to challenges, but don't necessarily come to a deeper understanding of their real being. Gurdjieff therefore insisted on this training method of the Feast of the Idiots as a way to develop the capacity to see the idiocy of oneself and others. Of course, there are other methods to discover and work with these essential patterns. But it sure is a lot more fun to do it with a good meal and Vodka! Also, we can loosen up much better in such an atmosphere, as opposed to the often strained experience of psychotherapy.

A key definition of someone who has attained Idiocy is that they are striving, and so in the process of becoming, or changing. Interestingly, this logic dictates that so-called "stationary beings" (Angels, for example), aren't Idiots. "There are twenty-one gradations of reason from that of the ordinary man to that of Our Endlessness, that is, God. No one can reach the Absolute Reason of God, and only the sons of God like Jesus Christ can have the two gradations of reason that are nineteenth and twentieth. Therefore the aim of every being who aspires to perfection must be to reach the eighteenth gradation."[70]

The Ladder of Reason[71]

1. Ordinary Idiot
2. Super Idiot
3. Arch Idiot
4. Hopeless Idiot
5. Compassionate Idiot
6. Squirming Idiot
7. Square Idiot
8. Round Idiot
9. Zigzag Idiot
10. Enlightened Idiot
11. Doubting Idiot
12. Swaggering Idiot
13. Authentic Idiot (also called "Born Idiot")
14. Patented Idiot
15. Genial Idiot
16. Polyhedral Idiot
17. Master Idiot
18. Perfect Idiot
19. Holy Idiot
20. Cosmic Idiot
21. Unique Idiot

"The special force of the Science of Idiotism as a method of instruction lies to a great extent in the ordering of the Series. Looking at the first ten - those most commonly toasted - there seems to be an ascending order from Ordinary to Enlightened. The next seven move in a direction that does not seem to be upward or downward, but rather of greater helplessness and dependence on influences out of their control. I doubt whether anyone studying the descriptions only would discover for himself the inner significance of the series. This lies in the fact that there are two directions of movement - "upwards' towards number twenty-one and "downwards" towards Ordinary Idiot. Since the ultimate aim and purpose of the existence of every being must be to approach as closely as lies within his power the Source of Everything that exists, one would naturally expect that to "mount" the scale is better than to "descend". The point is that to mount with encumbrances must sooner or later result in failure to move further. By the time a certain degree is reached, the encumbrances can no longer be shed, and they become an insurmountable obstacle."[72]

Gurdjieff urged a practical caution, making it clear that it is sometimes a good idea to revert back to the Ordinary Idiot as a way to cut one's identification with the special peculiarity of a particular Idiot – a tricky thing.[73]

Micheline Stuart, who has been in the groups of Maurice Nicoll, a pupil of Gurdjieff and Ouspensky, states in her book, *The Tarot-Way to Self Development,* that the Tarot contains a hidden theory of the evolution of man. The steps are designed to show people what is to be expected on one's individual path and what has to be striven for. "Only the highest effort counts. Compliance and half-heartedness are not enough. At every moment our efforts can change into the opposite. Therefore we must stay awake."[74]

It seems to me that an interesting parallel can be drawn between the Idiot Typology and the Greater Arcane of the Tarot, although we have already seen that such comparisons of diverse systems can raise problems. To identify the "Ordinary Idiot" as the "Fool" of the Tarot seems evident; however, to find comparisons with the geometric row (Square, Round etc) of the Idiots is more difficult. It could be (assuming that Gurdjieff's statement that the "Science of Idiotism is very old"[75] is correct) that the knowledge of the Idiots was incorporated into the

Renaissance Tarot but has, over time, endured changes in symbols and meanings. The following comparisons between the symbolism of the Tarot and the Idiots are presented merely as food for thought for the reader.

Usually the Tarot decks are numbered sequentially, starting with "The Fool" (No. 0) through "The World" (No. 21). The steps are interpreted in accordance with this sequence. But if we interpret the cards as a symbolic path of personal evolution, it seems to make more sense to reverse the sequence, starting with "The Fool", and then going further with "The Judgment" (No. 20) and ending up with "The Magician" (No. 1). Suddenly we have clear parallels with the Idiots. Of course, the Tarot contains images from the Renaissance and words from a bygone era, such as "High Priest" (or Pope), "High Priestess", or "Sovereign" (Monarch, King, Queen). To understand these images from the point of view of contemporary human development, I will rename them in the descriptions which are about to follow.

The Greater Arcane of the Tarot has 22 cards and images (often shown in connection with the Hebrew Kabbalah and the 22 letters of this language), while Gurdjieff's Idiots typology contains only 21. "The World" card, usually No. 22, seems to be of a different order. Therefore, I propose that we study it separately. If we then begin our sequence with the natural correspondence we will see how everything fits.

Within the card "The World", we see an encircled human being and the symbols of the four evangelists / animals of the apocalypse (bull, lion, eagle and angel), symbols which embody the "complete school of life". Each of these figures represents a center, or brain, of man: moving center, feeling center, thinking center; the angel symbolizes intelligence (the higher intellectual center) while the woman in the middle symbolizes love (the higher emotional center). Gurdjieff used this image of "The World" as the title illustration of the prospectus for his "Institute for the Harmonious Development of Man" (see picture). Here the angel is the central part of the design with the dove in the center, symbolizing the higher emotional center, and the eagle above, symbolizing the higher intelligence. In the center of the circle interwoven with the angel we also find the enneagram as a symbol of transformation. And, in his tale *Beelzebub's Tales to his Grandson*, this image was the logo of the Akhaldan-Society. But there is a difference: In his allegory, standing in front of their temple was the Sphinx. But instead of a human head, were the breasts of a virgin. Gurdjieff has given us another riddle to solve - we must be passionate in our search.

"Gurdjieff's Science of Idiotism is about the transformation, step by step, from the mechanical sameness which really is an absence of identity, to the other sameness which is the perfection of identity. One of the perils of this path is that one can take oneself as having a kind of identity, a kind of reality that one has not got. Living with this illusion, one may arrive at a point where it is impossible to get any further."[76]

5. The Ladder of Reason

"My experience has shown that anyone who sincerely follows the way of the spiritual world also become a better and more effective person in the natural world."
John G. Bennett

Of course, the Idiot's typology can be applied in understanding traits of people you have to do in daily life. But it makes a great difference, if you *see* your characteristics by yourself in the setting of the ritual, because then you can do something about it! Therefore, if you read the following descriptions and you don't "work at yourself" it may be entertaining to read and you also may get some new insight, but the deeper understanding can be missed if you haven't discovered one of the traits consciously within yourself.

In the following descriptions I'm using the masculine term, but of course "all sexes" are meant.

1. The Ordinary Idiot
People take for granted the idea of "ordinary" or "normal". But with humans there really is no normalcy at all. Each individual has something "not normal" - a special individuality. Therefore, I came to wonder, "What exactly is an 'Ordinary' Idiot?" If a person has embarked on a path of self-transformation, nothing is ordinary again. He is a "Fool", as in the Tarot card that represents this Idiot. He is a daydreamer, looking up into the sky while at the verge of an abyss. Only the dog, a symbol for the animal, physical side of man, is aware of this predicament.

The paradox is that only a fool will start on a Path not knowing where it leads, which is the only way to start down this path. Therefore, the Ordinary Idiot is the starting point for the growth of understanding, because he looks with the eyes of a child, an attitude that will allow him to avoid many hindrances, such as pre-conceived notions, on the way. He initially has the important capacity to see everything from a fresh perspective - until he has traveled for a while and becomes fixated on certain ideas about the path. This is the reason that Gurdjieff insisted on the idea of going back to the Ordinary Idiot if one became stuck at any given point. "Zen-spirit is beginner's spirit" one master said.

A classic example of the Fool is seen in the Oriental Mullah Nasruddin (a type that can be found in all cultures), in the many simple, funny stories in which he is struggling with life's persistent problems. In *Beelzebub's Tales*, Gurdjieff often referred to the Mullah, illustrating the qualities of simplicity, clarity, conscientiousness, humble responsibility and the absence of self-deception. These are the qualities of the Ordinary or Simple Idiot.

The Russian word "Obyvatel", the good and honest house-holder – in old Russia usually a craftsman or a peasant, nowa-days used for "the good citizen" - in Ouspensky's *In Search of the Miraculous*, also seems to correspond with the Ordinary Idiot.[77] To become an Ordinary Idiot, i.e. starting on the path one has to be grounded and settled in life with "normal" tasks to do. Only thinking and daydreaming doesn't lead further. The dog of the animal nature should get some attention.

It is clear that we need to retreat (actually rise up) to the level of the Ordinary Idiot if we are to circumnavigate the many obstacles on our path to self-development. "Gurdjieff in the *Science of Idiotism* insists on the necessity of returning to the point where we completely accept that we are the same as other people. That is meant by Ordinary Idiot."[78] If we don't begin from here, we sooner or later are caught in our own fantasies of doubt or grandeur, and it will be difficult to escape our own prison. At this point we should be naked, having no baggage to take with us.

Teaching Story: A simple man visited the Zen master, Baso, in China. "What are you looking for?" Baso scolded. "I'm looking for enlightenment," responded the simple man. The master responded, "You already have your own treasury chamber. Why do you look for it somewhere else?" "I don't know about this chamber. Where will I find it?" Baso answered, "You have it already - just turn inward." The man became enlightened and then traveled around declaring, "Open your treasury chamber and use its treasures."

Tarot: The Fool. This man (or woman) has packed his little bundle and is starting on his pilgrimage. He is led by his inner being. But as he is new on the path and very carefree, he can fall into many traps. He still doesn't know where his path will lead him and whom he can trust. He still lives in the Now, without thoughts about yesterday and tomorrow. Only a dog – his animal nature, the connection to the material world - can stop him from falling into the abyss and helps him to keep his common sense. Without this connection to the material world he can rapidly turn into a "candidate for a mental asylum" as Gurdjieff put it. With this he means all the people who lose themselves in fantasies about the spiritual worlds; these types of people are destined to fall into the traps of all kind of ideologies. The Ordinary Idiot must learn to look into the eyes of reality. "Work on oneself" is really "hard work" – the translation of the Chinese term Kung-fu, the martial art, which is in essence work on oneself, too.

Positive Aspect: Because he has the wish to become more than 'just normal', the Ordinary Idiot genuinely works on himself and is able to develop further.

Negative Aspect: Because he still has one foot planted in "normal" reality and doesn't want "to be a fool" or is perhaps afraid of seeming (or actually becoming) "crazy", he may lose his wish to pursue his path further. If we remain on the level of the Fool, we remain childish and immature. For the rest of our life this will be our state, regardless of whether we are successful in normal life.

2. The Super Idiot

I have led many ritual meals, and never has anyone ever proclaimed themselves to be a Super or Complacent Idiot, as I call this person, too. This is probably because, while participating in a spiritual group, no one wants to "out" themselves as being self-satisfied. This is, of course, due to their Chief Feature. However, I have met many people who become quite complacent after entering a spiritual path, allowing the revelations of the first few steps to create a dangerous sense of "already being there". Through the process of learning to think and to see in a new way, the Complacent Idiot begins to feel "special", knowing that he has something unique hidden within. But this feeling of being "special", regardless of its validity, becomes an expression of this Idiot's complacency, of his personality. It is typical for such an Idiot that he very frequently attends seminars for "self-development" of any flavor. Some of these Idiots travel great distances (for instance to Mongolia or Nepal) just to drink tea with Shamans, attending one of their rituals, and boasting afterwards that they know everything about shamanism. Another example would be one of these types of Idiot visiting the ashram of a famous Indian guru and, having received a blessing from him, feeling "chosen" or, even more dangerously, feeling enlightened or able "to do".

Everybody else sees that such an Idiot's complacency and arrogance are based on imagination, whereby he fantasizes having reached a high level of spiritual growth. However, this Idiot's essence is not even touched at all by any of this. He is far removed from real inner growth. His problem is that he has deceived himself into thinking he can "do", meaning that he is still under the illusion that he knows and understands, and has control over his functions. The Complacent Idiot is the "typical" quasi-intellectual who always thinks he knows better than everybody else, and looks down on the "Ordinary Idiot" for being, well, ordinary. But the world cannot function without the Ordinary Idiot, who sees to it that the market opens and the dogs are fed and the clocks are wound, without notice or reward. On the other hand, the Super Idiot can also make his way through life, an important quality and skill, and, if he can use this ability to further his inner development, he will have some use for the Work.

Teaching Story: One day a studied theologian called to set up an appointment to come over and interview me. He said that he wanted to learn more about the Gurdjieff teaching. When he came, I offered him coffee, sat down and asked him what he wanted to know. At this point, he began to explain to me everything he knew from the books on the subject of Gurdjieff and Ouspensky and quoted several texts by rote. This went on for an hour. Finally, he looked on his watch, thanked me profusely, and told me he had to go, stating that he was sure I could tell him many new things.

 *Tarot:* "The Judgment": A human being does not just awake suddenly to being balanced. Instead, hard work is necessary for him to awaken from his sleep, from the "death bed". On this level, we must all shed the clothes of our self-deception. We must become aware of all misconceptions and erroneous feelings about ourselves. The angel on this card calls you and sends you power, so that you will be able to work on yourself. Only if you are able to accept this help, which is offered by a Work group lead by an experienced teacher, can you hope to develop further.

Positive aspect: Although deep within him lies real substance, unless he can discover and admit to himself that his character is transitory and that his soul is undeveloped, he cannot proceed. If he can accept the weakness of his position, only then can he make progress.

Negative Aspect: As he has already achieved recognition based on his boasting, he falls into a trap of his own making which perpetuates his self-delusion and conceit.

3. The Arch Idiot
Gurdjieff loved the prefix "arch", as in "Archbishop", "Archangel", "Arch devil", etc. As his father was a Greek and Gurdjieff was fluent in that language, he also knew the meaning of the Greek work *árchein*: to begin, being the first, or being a leader. He used it in this sense for the Arch Idiot, the original Idiot. So here we have an archetypical Idiot who is neither ordinary nor complacent.

From my experience, and from the description of the Idiot itself, I actually feel that "Pretending Idiot" portrays the meaning more clearly. This type of Idiot is pretending to be an Idiot, because, although he is on a spiritual path, he is not on his *own* spiritual path. He is in a terrible position, even worse than that of the preceding Idiot, because he is not even bathing in his own glory; he is bathing in the glory of someone or something else. The Pretending Idiot is a classic "devotee" and, whether justified by an honest sense of piety or not, believes everything his master tells him *unquestioningly*. This is, in fact, typical behavior for most people, who are anchored in their personalities and are constantly identified with spiritual pop stars, like the Dalai Lama, the Pope, or Gurdjieff. This type of Idiot doesn't have an adequate grasp of the essential ideas of his path, nor does he strive to comprehend these. A Pretending Idiot is characterized by the idea of someone who is impressed by external signs and portents, but who cannot understand that following religions or "ultimate" spiritual paths will do nothing to cover up his own nothingness.

This Idiot type always tries to get into the inner serving circle of someone who has a prominent position either in life or in spiritual groups, a master or a guru. He deceives himself that the radiance of his master could be a substitute for his own radiance.

Teaching Story: Once upon a time, a young man thought, "If it were possible to experience different phases of life, I could avoid living unconsciously and ignorantly. I could come to understand age, and go through life already understanding its lessons."

By fate or coincidence he met a wise old man, who told him about a certain magical plant that had power over time and space, which would allow the young man to travel through time to experience himself at different ages. The young man found the plant and partook of it. He traveled first to his middle age, where he experienced a life full of hard work, a nasty wife and crying children. Quickly, he decided to get out of there and to proceed to old age. However, he found this to be much more boring than he had anticipated, as he was lying sick in an old peoples' home.

So he again partook of the plant, to return to his youth, but in doing so, he forgot everything he had experienced.

Then he thought of another experiment; to transform himself into another person. But he found this to be useless to his goal of experiencing himself better, because he found he could only experience this other person.

Having returned to his original state and age, he considered his experiences. He found that the most valuable part of his journey had been that it was different than what he had expected. He met the old sage again, who said, "Now that you know that it is not about the experiences that you want, but rather about the experiences you need, you can start to learn."

Tarot: "The Sun". The image is of a pair of twins, which illustrates the two sides to this level of idiocy or reason. On the one hand, because he is basking in the radiance of his boss or spiritual master(s), he imagines himself to have already climbed to a higher level of development, and to have his own place in the sun. On the other hand, if the Arch Idiot is able to realize his situation and commences to work on himself, he will be able to develop some real inner power and charisma of his own. The picture of children also shows that with a "beginner's mind" the person can get fresh energy from the sun, the strength to proceed on the path. The sun shows him the possibility of reaching a world of light, which he can also make his own.

Positive Aspects: He has recognized the gulf between his outer roles or positions and what he really is, which creates an uncomfortable feeling of inner hypocrisy. This insight will provide the motivation to work harder on himself.

Negative Aspect: He successfully blocks all feelings of contradiction, and remains stuck in his role of perpetual supporter. This is especially true if he is any good at his role, feels flattered, and subsequently begins to develop false pride in his role.

4. The Hopeless Idiot

After having struggled with flattery and pride, and having recognized one's elevated Ego, it seems one should be able to move up the ladder of reason. However, this process is not as easy as it sounds. In referencing the Hopeless Idiot, Gurdjieff always spoke with greater intensity because, having arrived at this point of the path, we will find another stumbling block which corresponds to an emotional response to reality. René Zuber reports, "The fourth toast to 'the health of all Hopeless Idiots' had been accompanied by an extensive commentary which the *tamada*, the director, had to repeat word by word even then, if he couldn't understand it deeply enough..." J.G. Bennett adds the following, "The details of the Hopeless Idiot were changed somewhat during the time that I went to meals at Number 6",[79] but the final form was fixed for many months before Mr. Gurdjieff died. It ran: "To the health of all Hopeless Idiots, subjectively and objectively. That is to say, to the health of all Hopeless Idiots who are destined for an honorable death and to the health of all Hopeless Idiots who are candidates for perishing like dogs."

Gurdjieff used – I think - the word "hopeless" in the sense of "lacking hope". Hope is a quality of Faith, as in "I hope for redemption". I would argue, then, that Hope is a passive attitude to life, which is only useful if you want to undertake something sensible and hope it will bring some gain. For example, if I invest in a company, I "hope" its value will double.

Hope also is part of the triad, "Faith, Hope, and Love". If the Hopeless Idiot corresponds with the Hope of this sequence, then perhaps the Arch Idiot corresponds with "Faith" (or "Belief"), and the next Idiot, the Compassionate Idiot, corresponds with "Love". Interestingly, Gurdjieff implied in the chapter of Ashieta Shiemash in *Beelzebub Tales*, that these three values, while forming the core of certain religions, aren't enough anymore. Interesting that there is also a sequence which goes "Faith, Hope and Charity", and it would not be unreasonable to associate the Compassionate Idiot which follows with Charity.

There are two subtypes of the Hopeless Idiot – the subjective and the objective. Of course, everybody would prefer to be this Idiot subjectively! The objectively Hopeless Idiot uses the daily work, in fact spirituality in general, as a strategy to avoid it. He is always occupied with something, takes on all possible difficulties, and does everything the teacher asks him to do. In this way he risks falling into the same trap as the Arch Idiot. He thinks he is working on himself, while merely doing the difficult tasks set to him by his master without complaint. He actually hasn't yet identified his individual task in life. To be a subjectively Hopeless Idiot, one must have begun to work on oneself seriously – and on one's own. Gurdjieff used this toast on every occasion to emphasize this point, and also that, "everyone must have an aim. If you have not an aim you are not a man. This is a very simple aim - not to perish like a dog. Everyone can have this aim. It is not a big aim. It is a small aim. But if you achieve this aim - to die honorably - then you can perhaps set yourself a bigger aim".

J. G. Bennett further states, "The inescapable force of this presentation was immeasurably enhanced by the deep seriousness with which he spoke. To hear it reiterated day after day was to have something driven into the depths of one's consciousness. One dare not shirk the issue: 'Unless you work you will inevitably perish'." Of course, with an honorable death he doesn't mean to die on the battlefield of war but rather to fight on the "battlefield of self realization". With the phrase "to perish like a dog" the dog of the first Tarot card "The Fool" comes in again - the animal nature. If you only follow everything that you are told, you don't really work on yourself and you are rather like a dog that follows the orders of his master.

In my eyes, an objectively Hopeless Idiot always follows every seemingly "important" teacher, guru, schools of thought and ideologies. He collects "papers" or CDs of all talks at "important" conferences and stocks them up in his archives. He is a typical "activist" always engaged in "absolutely important and necessary" activities, but all this work is external.

A subjectively Hopeless Idiot behaves similarly, but his essence is touched by these activities until one day he/she notices that the outer activities and worldly things don't really count. He has mastered the animal nature of himself. Then he is no longer hopeless.

Teaching Story of the "Objectively Hopeless Idiot": Nasruddin sat in an empty performance hall. The warden came along and said, "Why do you sit here? There is no show coming up." Nasruddin replied, "One day a big master will come and give Darshan. When this happens, I will be here already and be very near to him as well. Therefore I wait."

Teaching Story of the "Subjectively Hopeless Idiot": A Zen pupil asked his master: "Why do we have to get up every morning, put on our clothes, having breakfast and doing our work afterwards? Isn't there any possibility to escape this routine?"

The master confirmed to the pupil: "Yes, we clothe ourselves, we eat and we work."

"I don't understand this", the pupil insisted.

"If you don't understand, then put on your clothes, eat and do your work."

Tarot: "The Moon". We must have an aim in life to be ready to develop our essence. If we don't work towards an aim, we are "food for the moon", in contrast to feeding our own essence, and completely dependent on external influences. Only if you work on yourself are you able to escape the world of fantasies, symbolized by the moon. Stop identifying with your fantasies about yourself, your false image, which doesn't have any reality. Everybody has the potential for development, and can hope to transform into a "real human being". But to achieve this, you must develop the ability of impartial self observation instead of howling at the moon like the dogs in the picture. The powers of the unconscious, symbolized by the crab, impede us very often by making us cross "Lethe", the river of forgetfulness. Everybody who tries to liberate themselves from the attraction of the artificial light of the moon will be pursued by the howling dogs of societal pressures and constraints – material promises and temptations – which reinforce our illusions.

Positive Aspect: This Idiot feels hopelessness, even despair. Therefore, he proceeds with the work of aiming to achieve

74

freedom; of not dying like a dog, but of developing instead an immortal soul. With humility, he gives himself to the call of his "Real I".

Negative Aspect: This Idiot is complacent in his hopeless feature, which he sometimes recognizes in himself. He identifies with his successful attainment of bits and pieces of real knowledge, although he does nothing with them.

5. The Compassionate Idiot

I've seen many people traveling on a spiritual path who are very empathetic and/or compassionate. They think they should love everybody, and are very emotional about everything. Because they think that every creature is God's creature and should therefore be loved, they often resort to vegetarianism. However, they don't see, perhaps they don't want to see, that the whole of evolution is built on the feeding of and on other beings - "reciprocal maintenance", as Gurdjieff called it. This doesn't imply that one ought not to be compassionate or that one should kill other beings, but Compassion should be an inner, essential urge and not a moralistic or emotional thing. Love or Charity and Compassion can only arise if we have discovered our connection to the real spiritual dimension. It is not emotional in the way that we normally perceive emotions. Gurdjieff illustrated this distinction with two categories of compassion: "sympathetic" (really compassionate and acting invisibly) and "antipathetic" (disagreeable, without real feelings). Later on, he introduced a third category, "so and so", for people who are neither "fish nor flesh", whose sympathy for other people is superficial. This kind of person may eventually have an emotional response, but won't do anything about it. "To illustrate [the Compassionate Idiot] Mr. Gurdjieff told the story of the man lying starving by the roadside.

The true Compassionate Idiot will give his last crust to help him. But the Antipathetic Idiot will look around to see if someone is watching him. 'Perhaps fiancée or fiancée's father is watching from the window. Then he will give his last crust. If no-one is watching he will quickly go away. Perhaps even kick him. I hate such Idiots'," John G. Bennett reports.

The Compassionate Idiot, "so and so", sometimes gives and sometimes doesn't, "it depends on the weather". I think the following Zen story describes the situation well: One day, a pupil came to the master and complained, "Master, I have no control over my moods. How can I heal them?" "Show it to me," the master said. "I cannot show these moods at the moment." "When are you able to show them?" "They arise very spontaneously," the pupil replied. "Then," the master said, "These moods cannot be your real nature."

Contrary to the Hopeless Idiot, who is centered only on himself and always wants be at the center of the action, the Compassionate Idiot is concerned with other people. Unless he deceives himself, he realizes that he can only help others if he has attained a certain degree of inner being.

Teaching Story to the sympathetic Compassionate Idiot: A famous Japanese artist always insisted that his drawings and paintings should be paid in advance. Therefore he was called a "miserly artist".

When he received an order from a rich geisha, he asked for the highest price ever.

The geisha said to her master: "All this artist wants is money. His paintings are good, but his spirit is dirty. Money has spoiled him."

Later on, it emerged that the reason he was only after the money was that the province where he lived had been struck by an extreme famine. With the money he received for his pictures he built up stores of grain, so that in the future nobody would have to go hungry anymore.[80]

Teaching Story to the antipathetic Compassionate Idiot: At the edge of a pond, Nasruddin was about to fall in. A friend was close by and was able to prevent him from falling. Every time they met afterwards, the friend reminded him of his heroic act. After several of these encounters, Nasruddin casually brought the man to the pond again. At this moment Nasruddin jumped into the pond. With only his head above the water Nasruddin said, "Now I am as wet as if you hadn't caught me last time. Please don't mention your act again."

Tarot: "The Star". In the picture, we see a large star surrounded by seven smaller stars. The large star is our sun, the power of intelligence, while the seven smaller stars are the planets, symbols of human understanding. The glow of the stars is radiating over devoted nature, symbolized by the woman in the picture. The water is a symbol of the abundance and fertility of compassion, which nature gives freely.

It is clear that only through self-knowledge are we able to practice compassionate acts. You must learn to give away freely what you have received. The stars (i.e. our conscience) guide us on the path, so that we can emanate these qualities to the world around us. The stars are also the light which is guiding our newly acquired wakefulness. If we endured the trials of the night (having escaped the influence of the moon) the soul can wake up to the real life and is able to grow. Later on, it will lead the seeker to higher levels of spiritual attainments.

But to be able to receive the light, we must free ourselves of all the desires of personality and self-love. The pure water of life can only flow fully and unite with the flow of love if we have overcome egoistic motives by means of a lot of attention and effort on our part. We do not strive for worldly success any more, but for the growth of our being. We become aware that real compassion is only possible through selfless action.

Positive Aspects: He really has compassion from his heart and can see the suffering of others. If he acts from a base of real compassion (and not from his own self-serving ego) then he is able to help other people.

Negative Aspects: His compassion strokes his own ego and strengthens his self-love. He becomes blind to the real needs of people despite his genuine caring.

6. The Squirming Idiot

The Squirming Idiot is not able to recognize that he has already found an inner thread to his being. He works on himself, but at the same time he is afraid of the spiritual impact he sometimes feels. As in the corresponding Tarot card, "The Tower", the walls he has built around himself are struck by lightning, causing everything he knows to crumble. He is not yet able to bear the impact of the spiritual realm. On one hand, he has worked hard to achieve this level, but on the other, he is really afraid of the things that await him.

This Idiot tries to avoid sacrificing "normal" life, the image he has of the world. Yet he wants more. So he squirms between the two worlds and thinks he is really clever. "He will not realize that he is an Idiot", Gurdjieff said. "This Idiot comes to me and asks me for help. I prove him what kind of Idiot he is. He agrees: he's an Idiot. Then he leaves me and ponders: 'But why am I an idiot? Didn't I buy something for 100 Dollars and sold it for 200?

Therefore I'm not an idiot, Gurdjieff is an idiot." Gurdjieff despised the cleverness of this type, because they would fail to recognize the difference in scale of the two worlds around which they were skirting.

Simply put, this Idiot is embodied by the person (and we all know at least one) who always complains endlessly to friends about his sufferings, bad luck and strange experiences. He asks for advice but, despite everyone's best wishes, often including his own, he acts contrarily. Gurdjieff said of such a character, "He is like fish out of water. Fish knows that he cannot live without water. He has only a little time to get back into the water. But he has no legs. If I pick him up to put him back in water, he squirms and falls out of my hand so I cannot help him".

J. G. Bennett explains, "In both cases the Squirming Idiot is difficult to help. The conflict is now both in the inner and the outer world. The Squirming Idiot cannot find peace in either. He has not faith nor is he hopeless. He is not compassionate for he is too much occupied with his inner world. And yet he struggles. He is not satisfied. Even when he refuses to believe that he is an idiot, he does not trust his own judgment, but goes back to convince his teacher. His positive merit is that he struggles, and out of this struggle something will result."

Teaching Story: A wise man had two pupils. The first was always argumentative; the second was very quiet and introverted. For weeks and years, the first one objected to the master's words and instructions. Often he misunderstood what the master was saying, but still he went on asking questions and arguing with the answers. One day the old master came into the room, in which both students were drinking tea with an acquaintance. The wise man suddenly pointed to the quiet one – who at this moment became enlightened, his face a radiating glow.

"Look at this," said the friend to the talkative pupil, "Had you behaved similarly and not paid so much attention to your master, you would also have become enlightened long ago." But the pupil objected to his friend also, "The master could have done something to me, too, but who would have been able to urge him to do so?"

Tarot: "The Tower". Our ego, the tower, must be "struck by lightning", because otherwise there is no help possible. If you get struck with spiritual insight, the ego, your personality, might not be able to take it as enlightenment but as destruction. You will fear that you will lose command in "normal" life, or will become crazy. Everything you have fantasized and believed about yourself is crumbling and is becoming worthless. In the light of the higher powers you are nothing. You have to build up inner strength and a wish to overcome the bonds to the personality and therefore give up the clinging to the material world, which is the tower you have built yourself. You have to give up all false securities. So at this stage, the shock of the lightning can strengthen your decision to move on. Take this opportunity and stop looking for excuses in order to avoid the impact of inner transformation.

Positive Aspect: With sudden insight, he recognizes that his only hope will be trust in the guidance of his "Real I".

Negative Aspect: He cannot bear this help because his personality squirms like a fish and doesn't recognize that there is help or that he needs it. He is in between two worlds or caught between two stools…

Excursus: The three centers of gravity in human beings

In Gurdjieff's terminology, man has three centers of gravity for his perception of reality. The main focus of the first type is the moving center, connected to the brain stem. This person perceives the world mainly through the filters of his senses, and has a strong bond with material reality and objects. The second type perceives mainly through the feeling center, the limbic system, the diencephalons. This type is more sensitive to other beings and nature, but will very easily react emotionally. The third type judges his perceptions by his intellectual capacities, his thinking center, associated with the neo-cortex.

It goes without saying that this classification is only a starting point for the understanding of perception and behaviors. The three brains are interwoven with each other and have many different functions. Humans consist of a complex perceptive network. Thus, a moving type can also be sensitive, and a feeling type can also have a good intellect. But each type has his special filter which colors his perception, so that we can say that although everybody has three (or more) brains, the center of perception for any given person is generally more rooted in one of the centers than in the others – even if we have synchronized the brains by the "movements" and other inner exercises.

In reference to the "Science of Idiots" we can therefore state that the "Idiots" always come in groups of three on different levels. For example: the Ordinary Idiot has his center of gravity in the moving center, the Super Idiot in the feeling center (on his low level rather more emotional) and the Arch Idiot in the intellectual center. There is also the possibility of seeing an Idiot Type who is quite mixed, but still shows his type through his habit of acting from one center.

On the next level we have the Hopeless Idiot, rather more connected to the material world – shown by his drive to collect rather than to work on himself, or the Compassionate Idiot, centered in the feeling center, and the Squirming Idiot, centered in the intellect but unable to decide. Of course, the Squirming Idiot can have some compassion too, but even then he will be unable to decide what is right, probably he will be a Compassionate Idiot "so-and-so".

The following three Idiot Types fall into the category of geometric symbols: square, round, and zigzag. Here we can also observe the center of gravity: the Square Idiot is principally bound to matter, or moving center, the Round Idiot is predominantly a feeling type and the Zigzag Idiot is a typical intellectual.

I tried it as a little thought experiment : if you place the groups of threes on the points of the hexagram in the enneagram, starting with point 1, you will discover interesting interconnections via the lines. If we place the last three Idiots at point 4, we can clearly see how an Ordinary Idiot can develop into a Square Idiot, and so on. So this will throw some light on the enneagram typology which is used by psychologists. Since they usually place fixed personalities at fixed points, no real development is possible. With Gurdjieff's typology, by contrast, you can move along the lines if you transform yourself. And, if you put the last Idiots, 19, 20, and 21 at the point of the triangle you will see the influences and actions of higher powers on the transformation of human beings...

7. The Square Idiot

At this point in the progression, we reach the Idiots which are given geometric names: square, round and zigzag. Square is the symbol for earth, while round is the symbol for heaven. So what could "zigzag" mean? It seems like a spiral that is squaring the circle – or connecting earth with heaven, the spiral orbits of the planets around the sun. Of course there is a psychological dimension to it, but do not forget the cosmological aspect – as the saying goes: "As above, so below."

Gurdjieff explained, "The Square Idiot is he who is sometimes not Idiot. He is candidate for Round. The Round Idiot is always Idiot, but the Square sometimes has a moment of sanity." (This happens if he connects himself with the Ordinary Idiot again, if you use my example of the enneagram.) The Square Idiot eventually is not an Idiot when he stands in the corners. But what could this mean? If the Square Idiot centered in his moving center is sometimes not an Idiot, how could he be on his way to self-development? If he's not an Idiot, is he "normal"? The intellect of the Square Idiot is too materialistically orientated to be able to decide whether or not to go further into the realms that are outside of his ability to categorize in materialistic terms. He fears there will be no net to catch him, should he fall through the cracks of spiritual development. However, during moments of clarity, he pursues the adventure.

The common Square Idiot spends most of his time identified with things that aren't his to worry about. Sometimes he identifies with imagined things, sometimes with real things. But always he is identified with things that are "very important". This Idiot is always stressed and is constantly changing direction, rounding the corners furiously to follow another idea or have another opinion. However, it is at the corners that he can also slow down, either through the shock of need or a moment's clarity, at which point he can break free of the square and change the course of his life. The Square Idiot has great intellect - in his case for materialistic achievements like construction work or engineering - as well as practical abilities. He is very competent, able to organize things and repair gizmos. However he often uses his abilities for activities that don't help with his inner work. He comes to believe that his activities have objective value, and so loses touch with reality.

If the Square Idiot grasps his situation, even within the framework of his limitations, he can strive for a real aim. If he identifies with things and problems not of his own making, he is lost in his 'square-ness'.

The symbolism of Gurdjieff succeeds the psychological aspect. Traditionally the square is the symbol of matter. The Square Idiot is usually attached to the material world, while the following, the Round Idiot, a feeling center type, is connected to the spiritual world, as the circle is a symbol of the non-manifest, the infinite. But on this level the Round Idiot perceives the spirituality only through the filters of his feelings. This makes clear that the "Science of the Idiots" should also convey some spiritual teachings.

Teaching Story: A Zen-student asked his master, "What is the path?"
"The daily life is the path."
"Can you study it?"
"If you try to study it, you miss it."
The pupil was not satisfied and asked, "If I don't study, how can I know if it is the path?"
Enigmatically, the master responded, "The Path is not part of the world of perception, but it is also not part of the world of non-perception. Comprehension is a delusion, but not knowing is senseless. If you want to reach the path beyond all doubts, put

yourself into the state of freedom that heaven has. You would call it neither good nor bad."

This triggered the pupil and he was enlightened – he understood without understanding.

Tarot: This Idiot corresponds to the tarot card "The Devil", which expresses the illusionary personality, under the spell of the material world. Many different images and ideas of the devil exist, but the main idea is that he tricks us with illusions and binds us to a false and transitory world. If we awaken to the terror of the situation, we have the key to undo his shackles. "The Devil" is our personality, identified with the material world. If we work hard to free ourselves from the identification with the straight lines and the seemingly "solid" matter, we can escape our self-chosen prison. We should also see that the dualism between heaven and earth is a psychological concept, which in the case of the Square Idiot makes clear that the world itself doesn't have a fixed order. Only then will we be able to integrate the square of material things with the flow of the circle on a higher level of being.

Positive Aspect: He disciplines himself while he's in a corner, he can make a new decision that can set him on a fresh course. His insight remains intact and he becomes a Round or Zigzag Idiot.

Negative Aspect: He is unable to come to the right decision in a critical situation and he becomes trapped in his square-ness.

8. The Round Idiot

To transform into a Round Idiot is not the escape which it might appear; in fact it is quite the contrary, because the Idiot now finds himself "running in circles". He always sees things relatively, "in the round", and is not able to judge, distinguish or differentiate. His knowledge is quite extensive, but he isn't yet "himself", he has no identity of his own. He often understands things wrongly, and may express his thoughts in a confused or unclear manner. He says "A", but means "B". Gurdjieff once said that a Round Idiot is in an especially difficult situation because there is no place in the circle to slow down and get out (If you've seen or read "Meetings with Remarkable Men", you may recall the story of the Yezidi boy who was trapped in a magical circle; Gurdjieff freed him, just by creating an opening…). He cannot and will not take responsibility for himself or others, and this makes him feel lucky: whatever he does, nobody can blame him. He will say, "What do you expect? I am a Round Idiot'." Occasionally, he circles round and round at such a furious pace that he ends up being driven into hysterics. If he is lucky, he will escape the circle and become a Zigzag Idiot. But until and unless that happens, he stays one step ahead and one step behind. "Once Mr. Gurdjieff spoke of the Round Idiot more seriously," Bennett reports. "He said that he must struggle very hard and continuously: 'but he can do this because he is Round Idiot. If he sees his Idiotism he will struggle day and night to be free'."

As the circle is also a symbol for the whole, for perfection, and for heaven, a Round Idiot is an intuitive type, who has the capacity to think beyond the material realm. He is able to 'see things in the round' and to connect ideas. J.G. Bennett was a Round Idiot for a time, and is an excellent example. His intellectual strength was to "feel" the whole. So he developed the holistic method of Systematics, the patterns of interaction between each of the numbers (monad, dyad, triad, tetrad, etc).

The will to combine all of one's knowledge into a big picture is a great strength, which comes out of a feeling of inadequacy and a need to understand the whole.

If such an Idiot becomes aware of his inadequacy, he always will have a "reminding factor" within him, which will help him to work on himself in a way that others cannot. "Or he must marry", as Gurdjieff mocked, meaning that a partner can be a strong reminding factor, especially the wife, if I may state this as a man…

Teaching Story: A gardener discovered Nasruddin amongst his carrots in his fenced field and shouted, "What are you doing here? This is private property!"
Nasruddin remained calm. "A stormy wind blew me over the fence."
The gardener guffawed, "And how comes it that the carrots are torn out?"
Nasruddin calmly responded, "I guess that happened when I fell on the ground."
"And what do you have in your bag?"
"Hold on, don't make it too complicated. I, myself, was just wondering that!"

Tarot: "Temperance". This picture exemplifies this situation. The angel pours water from one vessel into another. This is a symbol for the eternal cycle but also of the possibility of renewal, which the Round Idiot has on this level. In fact, the card doesn't hint at "temperance" as such, but rather at the insight of the measure of all things, which you can only perceive when you have inner clarity. The "Guardian angel" shown on the card incarnates the help that we can receive to give our life new direction - if we are able to accept this help. The angel, the spiritual power of our being, pours the water of life into the vessel of our essence and enables us to find a new direction in our life.

Positive Aspect: As he works persistently on himself to get out of the vicious circle, out of his self-limiting perfection (the symbol of the circle), he may finally be able to erase a spot on the circumference of the circle, allowing himself a way out.

Negative aspect: The circle will become his jail. He is trapped in his perfect circle and is hypnotized by it. He is identified with his successes and doesn't find, or even recognize a need for, a way out.

9. The Zigzag Idiot

The Zigzag Idiot has broken out of the circle and has managed to shed his self-centeredness. He is traveling along a zigzagging spiral into unknown realms and in new directions, although he doesn't know where it all leads. He feels that he has overcome all kinds of orders and rules. This feeling, in which everything seems open and not subject to ordinary laws, is essentially a necessary precursor for becoming enlightened.

This Idiot was always dealt with in a jocular manner. The typical toast was, "To the health of all Zigzag Idiots, that is to say, to the health of all those who have five Fridays in the week; and to the health of all hysterical people and to the health of all three sexes." In this quote he is referencing a Russian idiom, "seven Fridays in a week"[81], which describes people who are unreliable and erratic, because they change their decisions all the time and don't keep their words or promises. A Zigzag Idiot never gets his work finished and is always on the brink of disaster. You can't trust him, because the Zigzag-Idiot has no real stability within himself. His defining quality is "extravert strength and introvert weakness". Even when he undertakes efforts he remains at the same place, relative to an upwards spiral. As he has no inner stability, he tends to sway between extremes, and can appear eccentric, extravagant, and wound up like a clock. Gurdjieff said, "I admire such Idiot. He makes many mistakes, but he never stop - day, night he struggle". We can see a similarity to the Squirming Idiot, but the Zigzag-Idiot has managed to find a line, even though this line is not straight. Impulsively he follows the ideas and urges that arise within him. If he can remember to use these frenetic changes of direction as a reminding factor, he can develop further.

Teaching story: A pupil of Zen had studied many years with a master and learned a silent meditation. After his master died he went to study under another. There he sat down and went into deep meditation. The master asked him, "What is the use of sitting still?" The pupil answered, "I want to reach Buddha-hood." After a while the master took a brick and started to polish it. The pupil became curious and asked, "What are you doing there?" The master replied, "I want to make a mirror from this brick." "Oh no," said the pupil, "you won't succeed at this!" The master then said, "You also won't reach Enlightenment by sitting still." "What should I do instead?" asked the pupil. "Do you want to become a master of meditation or do you want to reach Buddha-hood?" the master asked him. "If you want to reach Buddha-hood you must train your spirit and not sit around idly…"

Tarot: In the Tarot this Idiot corresponds to "Death". If the Zigzag Idiot can rid himself of his fantasies and imagination about life, death and beyond, he will find a straight line, continuity, and develop inner strength. He has to let go of his personality and die to himself. If, through the process of destruction and purification,  he enters a new level of being, then he will open up the space of new possibilities. The picture symbolizes the death of the worldly personality, sometimes also called "Ego", which is attached to material reality by intellectual considering. Now this Idiot is in a process of transformation from attachment to the material world into the world of being, and is searching for the opening to the powers of the spiritual essence. The wish for self -realization brings this Idiot to a new level, where he opens up new vistas of his life.

Positive Aspect: He has rid himself of his fantasies and imaginings, and he is on his way to overcoming his Ego and to finding his own path. It is through the death of his fantasies and imaginings that he has developed some inner strength which will help him to overcome his Ego and find his own path. He has used the pursuit of finding continuity on his path as a reminding factor, and so he can develop.

Negative Aspect: He is stuck with following his impulses, and loses himself in his own craziness. Even his impulse to work on himself is lost in the crowd of competing impulses.

The Zigzag Idiot is the last Idiot on the 'path of knowledge'. What follows are the Idiots who lie on the 'path of being'.

10. The Enlightened Idiot

If the Zigzag Idiot were able to take one step up on the "Ladder of Reason" he would suddenly feel enlightened. He takes a deep breath and envisions the panorama of a new world. But enlightenment is its own special trap, because a person who has reached this level is tempted to feel really "special", and that he or she "made it". This level is dangerous because it is not the end it appears to be, but really just another beginning, and humility is the only way out, either up or down. The Enlightened Idiot is at a critical and exciting juncture; he has laid within himself the foundation for becoming a "three-brained being"[82] and can now embark on the path towards becoming a Perfect Idiot.

The Enlightened Idiot "overcomes great difficulties in order to acquire not more information but real knowledge. This work changes him, and he climbs up the scale of Idiotism until he becomes Enlightened. Enlightenment is the beginning of the path of working from being and not personality. At this stage, a person knows everything that it is possible for him to know. He knows what he must do in order to reach real freedom. But he cannot do it."[83] This Idiot has reached a stage at which he cannot rely solely on his knowledge anymore - he must develop the parallel aspect of his *being*. He is "enlightened", but that can't get him any further, because it has been primarily an intellectual or visionary achievement, through the use of meditation, for example, and he has become identified with it and limited by it.

The Sufis distinguished between *"hal"*, a temporary vision or enlightenment, and *"makam"*, the level of being. For this reason, an "Enlightened Idiot" is a particularly problematic case because, in Gurdjieff's view, he has had insights into the "other reality", but hasn't yet got the stability of being which is necessary for further evolution. If he doesn't see his precarious position, "even God cannot help him", Gurdjieff once remarked.

The Enlightened Idiot has reached a dead-end street if he clings to his enlightenment. He feels called upon to be a spiritual teacher, maybe even feels qualified to be a guru, because he has definite insights into the spiritual realm. But to move on, he must leave behind everything that he knows and has acquired and return to the level of the Ordinary Idiot to obtain the renewed energy which comes from a certain innocence and naivety. He has to find a completely new way of seeing. He needs to find his "beginner's spirit" again.

Teaching Story: Master Kasan was asked to hold a talk for politicians and merchants. He hadn't done this before and had "stage fright".

As he came back to his house he called for his students. He explained that he had not been able to remain inwardly calm and relaxed. "Therefore," he said, "I will not be your teacher anymore." So he went out and found another master and returned to the position of student. After four years he went back to his own pupils, again as their teacher.

Tarot: The tarot card, "The Hanged Man", symbolizes the situation of the Enlightened Idiot. He is hanging by one leg, upside-down. The new perception is the opposite of the former way of seeing. Suddenly things are different. We can see that the Enlightened Idiot faces a significant dilemma. To develop the inner stability and depth needed for his evolution, he will need more than just the significant breadth of knowledge that he has accumulated. Something else is required. He must give up everything of his "own" and submit to a higher Will.

Positive Aspect: He recognizes that enlightenment is no personal achievement, but a gift. He recognizes and is grateful for what this grace has given him thus far. In humility, he is prepared to give up everything he knows in order to receive further help. He accepts his own nothingness.

"We must give up every pretense of being 'special' to reach real freedom", John G. Bennett once said.

Negative Aspect: His pride drives him to believe that he has achieved everything on his own force. His ego expands at an exponential rate, which crowds out any hope of his "Real I" finding room to exist in his heart. He is stuck in his enlightenment, and has the dangerous capacity to lead others into confusion.

11. The Doubting Idiot

"He that has understood himself, despairs of himself. He that despairs of himself, begins the path to self-realization, begins to see who he is," to paraphrase Philo of Alexandria. Gurdjieff said of this Idiot, "I like this Idiot. He doubts he Idiot and then he see." Rina Hands reports that she always was very puzzled about this Idiot. "For months I never heard anything mentioned except that he was 'shit of shit'. But then there were two kinds: one antipathetic - he only wishes to appear clever, and one 'sympathique' - he doubts sincerely. About this one: 'I like this Idiot - with him I will drink all night." Gurdjieff often used the terms 'antipathetic' and 'sympathetic'. 'Antipathetic' is disagreeable, without compassion. In the case of an Antipathetic Doubting Idiot, Gurdjieff despised his cleverness because he uses it to avoid facing the implications of his self-realizations. The

Doubting Idiot was sometimes compared with the Round Idiot, because they both move in circles, shirking responsibility and solid ground. But a Doubting Idiot also has certain strength of being. He is not like the Enlightened Idiot, who cannot doubt. He doubts, and so can question achievements and can therefore make room for growth.

A doubting person broods too much about himself and the world. Everything is questioned, faith, knowledge and the Work. He throws his doubt like a wet blanket, covering everything. If he can use this tendency as a reminding factor, he can find the courage to move forward.

Teaching Story: The master was in his best mood and said, "Were I to tell you everything I know and understand you wouldn't believe me. If I even were to tell you the biggest truth only understood by enlightened masters, you wouldn't be able to follow. Were I to prove to you that the world doesn't exist, you wouldn't believe me. And were I to unveil your eyes to peer behind the curtain of visible reality, you still would have doubts." After a pause, a woman from the public shouted loudly, "Do you really expect anyone to believe that?"

 *Tarot:* This Idiot corresponds to the tarot card, "Strength". Unless this person can find their inner strength to move beyond doubt, he will stand in his own way. His situation is a heart-breaking one, in that he doesn't trust himself and so projects doubt as a sort of protection. He must use strength and courage to work on himself further. If he accepts the real strength of being that he has developed, his inner lion is awakened. In this card, the symbol of infinity above the head of the woman shows us that his potential is infinite. The picture

94

challenges us to submit to the strength of our being and lastly to our "Real I" in the center of our essence. We must find new values und must leave indecision behind. The feminine, intuitive side in us is only able to tame the lion of doubt if we don't want to be eaten up by it as Jesus is reported to have said[84]: "Happy is the lion who becomes a human being, if he is eaten by man. Worry about a man, who is eaten by a lion and so the lion becomes a man."

Positive Aspect: This Idiot doubts honestly. He even doubts whether or not he is an Idiot. And as he doubts everything, he is not identified and is, therefore, able to see himself impartially. He has an aim to really understand what the path to perfection is about. If he can turn his urge to doubt everything into a capacity to discern 'what to doubt and when' (like the highly refined nose of a dog), then he can turn this weakness into a skill. This discernment comes from having the courage and strength to trust oneself.

Negative Aspect: He doubts, but his doubt is from fear or cleverness, and so he is identified with it, perhaps ironically seeing it as strength. He is clever and overestimates himself. He is stuck in his cycle of doubts and becomes cynical.

12. The Swaggering Idiot

By "Swaggering" - boosting oneself - Gurdjieff most probably meant the pride which can overwhelm a person once he has reached this level of development. On this level, you have created a new picture of the world. The problem is that you easily lose sight of the interconnectedness of things. Gurdjieff used the picture of a peacock as an example.

"One of the many specific features of the psyche of this strange bird is that the peacock, why I don't know, considers it always necessary to swagger, and thus will often for no reason whatever puff himself out. Even when nobody is looking at him he swaggers and puffs himself out, though he does so in this case exclusively because of his own imagination and silly dreams."[85]

Why did Gurdjieff place the boasting or swaggering on this high level of the ladder? As a peacock you open your beautiful plumage to show your glamour. This Idiot may do so because he has traveled far along the path. He has visions and is able to see the beauty of creation. But like the peacock, he loves to show off, demonstrating his level of being to anyone who will listen or watch. In a way, this Idiot is the counterpart to the Enlightened Idiot, because he has overcome his blindness and his doubts, but has reached a stage beyond the stagnation of the Enlightened Idiot. He must realize that his ego is a hindrance to real progress. The Swaggering Idiot is like a "guru" stuck halfway. He collects pupils like other people collect stamps, and he proclaims wisdom that he hasn't really come to understand.

If the Swaggering Idiot remorsefully realizes that he has occupied a place he cannot really hold, he has a chance of escaping from his prison of vanity and megalomania. He most probably will have to also descend to the stage of the Ordinary Idiot to re-experience life simply. Although he has worked at his being, has certain strength of character and is able to guide people, he is identified with his greatness.

Teaching Story: A pupil attended all of the seminars and talks by a renowned spiritual teacher, though he never asked questions or said anything.

One day the teacher asked the pupil to come into his private room. "For years I have given exercises and teachings, but I don't have the impression that you have made any progress."

"I'm happy that you noticed this," the pupil said, "because for some weeks I've had the feeling also that you're not working hard enough at it."

Tarot "The Wheel": The Swaggering Idiot who is not aware of his situation falls into the vicious circle that "The Wheel" of the Tarot illustrates. The energetic and inspired people who are taken up by the wheel are not always aware that after the zenith comes a descent. We must learn to see this totality and judge the situation correctly. We should connect with our roots again, so that we do not fly away into the void of imagination.

Positive Aspect: This Idiot is full of Pride and Vanity, but, at the same time, has a developed sense of self-reflection. If he can see his weaknesses, he can burn through them and rise like a phoenix from the ashes, to become a Remorseful Idiot.[86]

Negative Aspect: He behaves like a peacock. His Vanity is in control and he doesn't think that he is in a bad position or that he needs help. This feeling can even cause him to negate the power of grace, which is the only thing that can possibly help him through the critical next phase in his development. He sees his boasting and enthusiasm as strength, and so is hindered from finally being free of his ego.

****

Very seldom did Gurdjieff's toasts go beyond the first twelve Idiots. The following Idiots aren't easy to understand. These people have reached a higher level of being that is difficult to comprehend from an ordinary world-view. Their defining characteristics are hidden within the structure of their essence pattern. The next triad of Idiots, the Authentic, Patented and Genial, show the characteristic features of these people who are commonly referred to as "eccentric". These types exhibit signs of being more centered in their own individuality, however their problems lie in the possibility of becoming "fixed" at this stage. Only with will force, with the help of the Real Will of the Real I, can such a person climb further up the ladder of reason.

13. The Authentic ("Born") Idiot

A "Born Idiot", as Gurdjieff often referred to this Idiot, has reached a stage of integration so that he is based in his own being. He is "authentic", centered in his real being. This Idiot experiences a life defined by a new kind of freedom – he can feel how he wishes to feel, and do what he wishes to do; he can make choices from his unique individuality. His door to consciousness is wide open! However, at this level of being many fluctuations between thoughts and feeling, personality and essence, still exist.

Teaching Story: A sage settled in a hut a short distance from a village. He spoke not a word. Every day many people came to him from all over the world. They asked him questions, but he responded with silence. The village prospered, and the motels and restaurants did good business, so the villagers decided to bring good food to the sage every day.
The sage always ate it appreciatively. One day, they noticed that he hadn't eaten the meal from the day before.
Suddenly, the sage spoke, "You can take this away."
The people were astonished, "You've never spoken before!"
"Of course not," the sage answered, "The meals have always been excellent before."

Tarot: The corresponding Tarot card, "The Hermit", represents the idea of the Born Idiot. He carries his own light in front of himself. The danger of this stage is that it can easily become static, whereby he is no longer able to leave his self-imposed cave. But the picture also shows the necessary phases of conscious retreat, of contemplation, which are helpful to settle into one's essence so that it can grow undisturbed. We must obtain clarity about our situation at this stage, and we must meditate upon our wish if we are ready to climb up the ladder of reason.

Positive Aspect: The positive aspect of this Idiot is that he has humility, and knows that he doesn't know. To develop real self-knowledge, it will be important for this Idiot to realize the deeper levels within himself and to connect with his "Real I", which can guide him in his pursuit of further development.

Negative Aspect: While the Enlightened Idiot, the corresponding Idiot on a lower triad, has collected more knowledge than being, the Born Idiot rests in his being, and forgoes the pursuit of further knowledge. Therein lies the danger for this Idiot – he becomes self-content, and loses touch with the dynamics of life and of the search.

14. The Patented Idiot

Since English was not his native language, Gurdjieff occasionally used some peculiar terms. By Patented Idiot, he meant that this person has a "patent" to be an Idiot. More than just "Authentic", to have a "patent" one has to have worked really hard to achieve this thing of value: made the discovery, done all the paperwork, submitted the form for the claim, etc.

The Tarot card "Justice" associated with this Idiot shows us that now we have to find a balanced perception for the rightness of our decisions and actions. There is no difference between them – they must go together.

The Patented Idiot is even more strongly anchored in his being than the previous Idiot. He is skilful in mind, body and emotion, acts without hesitation, and is able to come up with innovative solutions. These practical talents are an indication of the connection he has established with his "Real I". Because of this, he is lulled into the belief that everything is easy; that he need simply open his mouth for food to fall in. He becomes lazy in his actions, in the sense that he ceases to reflect adequately on the value of his actions. He is emotional on a gut level, and therefore can easily fall prey to the trap of reacting to, instead of thinking through, situations. He is eloquent and cosmopolitan and knows what he is able to do. The Patented Idiot always thinks he is cleverer and more knowledgeable than other people, and often is, which traps him into his haughty sense of himself.

Teaching Story: Nasruddin decided to learn something new. He went to a famous piano teacher and asked, "How much is one lesson?" "In the first month you pay $100 per hour, in the second month $80, and in the third month $60." "Great," Nasruddin replied, "then I'll start in the third month."

Tarot: The card, "Justice", corresponds to this Idiot. Justice needs a balance between right and wrong, between scale and sword. Justice, then, is a sort of representative of the idea of God. This also brings in another idea: In order to be truly just, a judgment needs to have taken into account the totality of any given situation. Very often, however, a person cannot impartially judge

a situation because he is much too preoccupied with his own aims and is therefore "blind in one eye".

Positive Aspect: He correctly assumes responsibility for himself and others, but often his decisions are too "legalistic" in that he judges by intellectual assumption as opposed to sound reason (as the Ordinary Idiot eventually is able to). He can be "blind in one eye", unable to judge in a balanced way, but his sense of duty guides him intuitively to help him make the right decisions in the end. As a saying goes: "In the land of the blind, the one-eyed man is king."

Negative Aspect: He is clever to a fault. He takes pride in his abilities and becomes stuck in this role. This Idiot can also become too strict, and respond to others too critically, demanding perfection and not allowing for weakness.

15. The Genial Idiot
The last Idiot of this triad has qualities of being that seemed to elicit from Gurdjieff certain typical, critical responses: "Of stinking heredity", for example. This Idiot may hark from the upper classes, which affords him or her access to the education, sciences and financial opportunities for the pursuit of their spiritual path. Gurdjieff joked about this Idiot often, because this Idiot often brought with him a sense of entitlement that made him an easy target.

In our contemporary times, we should see the Genial Idiot as one who understands and has mastered inner transformation. He is relatively conscious of his internal and external worlds. In

Gurdjieff's terminology, he is "Man No. 5", though such an Idiot must continue to work on himself, as must any other person.

Genial Idiots are fully developed characters whose functions are well integrated. They are cosmopolitan and trans-cultural in their worldviews, and they have a clear aim. They are relatively conscious of themselves, and are able to make decisions or take corrective action without undue or inappropriate emotions. Their trap is that they think their path was made uniquely for them - custom-built, so to say, for their personal enlightenment. Every Genial Idiot also has a good part of frenzy in him. Most probably that is the reason why he was sometimes called "psychopath" - not in the forensic sense, but in reference to his identification with his specialty. My example for this type is the esoteric scientist, a British eccentric who studies the crop circles in England for twenty years because he believes that these circles are made by extraterrestrials. The borderline between the genius and the psychopath is thin. If such an Idiot is able to submit to the real spiritual force, the guidance of his "Real I", then he will make a good contribution to the evolution of humanity.

Note: The words "genius" and "genial" mean quite different things in English. I am not sure what G intended here, but a genius is a person of extraordinary intellect, whereas a genial personality is one which is amiable and pleasant. Obviously this idiot is not a genius in his idiocy, but still has some "blind spots" to overcome.

Tarot: The Tarot card, "The Chariot", illustrates this type of Idiot. The Chariot, the Warrior, has won control of his emotions, which are represented by the horses (on some cards these are illustrated as two sphinxes which symbolize the hidden wisdom). He is Arjuna of the Bhagavad-Gita, a warrior well-prepared by his heredity and education. He thinks victory on the battlefield is a mere formality, but in reality, there is no such guarantee. This

privileged person must keep his head about his, for fear of losing both battles – the battle for his external life and the one on the battleground of his internal work.

Positive Aspect: This Idiot has a global, trans-cultural, and trans-spiritual perspective. He has a clear aim, knows where he wants to go, can make and change decisions effectively, and takes criticism as a challenge.

Negative Aspect: His trap will be that he desires and only recognizes a very "special path", unique to him. For example, he could not tolerate joining a Buddhist monastery in which everybody looks the same and wears the same clothes. He looks instead for an "eccentric" spiritual path, like Kabbalah or Zen (not the monastic one), which he can adapt to an individualistic form of his own liking. He may be a successful scientist with spiritual inclination, but he may become identified with his achievements and will not take the next steps on the spiritual path.

*****

About the following Idiots, there are only a few hints or direct quotations from the Tradition. Except for No.17 the rest were never toasted, to the best of my knowledge. Nevertheless, using the symbolism of the Tarot will assist us in our attempts to grasp the possible meanings of these Idiots.

*****

16. The Polyhedral Idiot

One source mentioned that this Idiot was called "polyhedral" which means" many-sided". I think that this name is appropriate for this stage, because it corresponds to a higher level of the Geometric Idiots (Numbers 7, 8 and 9). The Polyhedral Idiot is not square, like the Idiot who runs blindly from one corner to the next, nor does he circle around himself, as does the Round Idiot. His difficulty lies in his ability to do so many things, and to experience so many possibilities. He is the "Master of the Glass Bead Game (Magister Ludi)" of Hermann Hesse's novel "The Glass Bead Game". The Magister Ludi works to discover the synergy between all known sciences and arts, and to connect the material knowledge with the spiritual. The Polyhedral Idiot lives like an isolated scholar in an ivory tower, studying all esoteric, spiritual and scientific knowledge, and works to give mankind a new understanding of the world.

The world is incomprehensible in its structure and meaning, but this Idiot is undaunted and seeks to explore and discover life's secrets. He is a visionary, in touch with the "higher intellectual center", and he will bring new ideas into the world. He is on the verge of becoming "Man No. 6".

Tarot: **In many decks you will find the card "The Lovers" at this place in the sequence. The Tarot has been reinterpreted repeatedly over time, so there is no telling whether or not the modern sequence is correct. The Polyhedral Idiot corresponds exactly to "The High Priest", also called "hierophant". A hierophant has been the teacher or priest of old Greek Eleusian mysteries. The aim of these mysteries has been initiation into the knowledge of**

extrasensory or transcendental realms. Some scientist says that for this purpose, a drink containing psychoactive mushrooms was ingested. Regardless of the truth of that, in my opinion "The Hierophant" also accurately symbolizes the "Magister Ludi". As in the book, *The Name of the Rose*, by Umberto Eco, he is the real Gnostic, the master of the library. His every action and decision is made on the basis of spiritual considerations, as opposed to worldly ones. To this Idiot, only the source of his intentions matter, so success or failure is of no concern. His essence is developed, and he takes on the responsibility of the "holy crown" (the pope's conical hat - called a "tiara" - shown on the card). In one interpretation[87], this hat has a phallic shape, being a sexual symbol of the ancient religions and able to symbolize the creative fruitfulness of this person.

Positive Aspect: This Idiot has a developed higher intellectual center and a direct perception of reality. He can experience a state of "cosmic consciousness". He emanates real compassion and love, and has deep humility before all spiritual powers and the creative intelligence in the evolution of life. But he knows he cannot hold on to these achievements, and also knows that he has to retreat on the "ladder of reason" to the center of the creative void, from which everything has emanated.

Negative Aspect: He becomes trapped in his wisdom and doesn't realize that, unbelievably, the path is not finished.

17. The Master Idiot

Gurdjieff once claimed himself to be an Idiot No. 17. The Master Idiot has attained everything a man can attain on this path. He has mastered himself and can lead humanity on a spiritual path. He has integrated compassion and love into himself, and so is free of egoism (the poison of the Enlightened and Swaggering Idiots). A good example of this Idiot is Jelaludin Rumi, the oriental Sufi mystic of the 13th century, whose teachings centered on Love and Compassion. In Buddhism, this type of person is known as a Bodhisattva, a human being who, after achieving immortality, chooses to reincarnate again in order to help all humanity.

Gurdjieff could never be induced to give a term for this Idiot. "Indeed, he said that no one would ever know it, because when we reach him in the toasts, 'I dance on the table, but no one sees, as they are all under the table drunk'."

Tarot: The Tarot card "The Lovers", which follows in our new sequence, shows that when the "higher" love fires its arrow into our heart, we are on our way to developing the most important quality of all - uncompromising love for the world and humanity. Pure compassion has overtaken us. We are in contact with our soul, symbolized by the feminine. But love also blinds.

According to Gurdjieff there are three forms of love:
Love of the body
Love of the feeling
And love of the spirit.

If we succeed at this stage in integrating and synchronizing all centers completely, we can love holistically and we will also have developed our total potential, the basis from which to climb the next step of the ladder.

Positive Aspect: If the Master Idiot recognizes that the "Path of the Heart" must be supplemented with the "Path of Objective Reason" he can become a Perfect Idiot.

Negative Aspect: The experience and manifestation of cosmic love is only one third of the cosmic power of Will; it must necessarily be accompanied by the active and creative power of "Doing", as well as the reconciling force of "Integration". The unification of these three cosmic forces was referred to in Chapter 2 as "Djartklom", but is also known as the Law of Three (or "Triamazikamno" elsewhere in *Beelzebub's Tales*). You will find this Idiot referenced to as "incarnations of love" in historical spiritual literature; Shams-i-Tebris and Jelaluddin Rumi are examples. But to be centered in Love and Compassion only is one-sided and therefore a hindrance to completeness.

18. The Perfect Idiot (or: "The Realized Idiot")

This leads to the stage of the Perfect Idiot, a role that a human being can seldom fulfill. "It was significant to me because it was the first time in my presence that he [Gurdjieff] has made the claim to be the 'Teacher of our Epoch' so clearly. Of course, Elizabeth has told me that he spoke about 'very few No. 18 ever exist - for example, Ashiata Shiemash was No. 18'."[88]

Ashiata Shiemash was presented by Gurdjieff in *Beelzebubs Tales* as a great spiritual teacher who had come to the realization that humanity could not evolve solely through the religions' virtues of faith, love and hope. He concludes that only the "holy impulse" of the conscience is able to awaken humanity from sleep. This conscience should not be confused with social morality. Conscience is an independent inner ability to judge; that which is able to see reality and to act correctly as circumstances dictate. No written rules can be comprehensive or flexible enough to be able to meet all changes and challenges of human life, but a functioning conscience can. Con-science is the knowledge which stems from the cosmic intelligence.

Tarot: "The Emperor" falls next in the sequence of the Tarot of the Middle Ages. He is able to judge and act impartially in both worldly and spiritual matters, and he is generally assigned the highest intelligence. In contemporary times, a mythical person like Ashiata Shiemash would be appropriate for this place; the root of the word "Ashiata" contains both "Asha" which means "law" and "Shah" which means king, which leads me to associate this Idiot with this Tarot card. On the picture of the card you see the king holding a scepter (again a phallic symbol for creativity), with a triadic cross (the three forces united) by his right hand. Beside his left hand is an eagle, the bird-symbol of holistic visions from above.

The danger, or negative side, of this stage is that power and authority can blind as well as command. Such a person can be intolerant, high-handed and violent. In such a case, a king must become a fool, an Ordinary Idiot again. Perhaps this was the role of the fool in the court of the king. Thus, even a person who has achieved this level of transformation ought to be open to the "beginner's mind" represented by the "Fool".

19. The "Holy" Idiot
The Holy Being (which can be woman or man alike) occupies a world beyond ordinary nature. They are often ascribed special powers and abilities – miracle workers. Holy Idiots are not

touched by the needs of the world, and their followers are devoted to them in pursuit of the smallest spark of their holiness. This Idiot has not arrived at this level by his or her own efforts, but has been touched by grace, has been "blessed". "A saint is a man or woman who is completely and permanently liberated from egoism. When such a being is ready, the spiritual power ... can enter into the soul and unite with it. Then the creative energy of the True Self is wholly guided and directed by the spiritual power. Such a soul can be the instrument for the working of miracles and for the spiritual awakening of others."[89] Examples are great mystics like Hildegard von Bingen, Teresa of Avila, Ramana Maharshi of Arunchala, Ramakrishna, Bahaudin Naqsband, among others.

Tarot: The Tarot card, "Empress", represents this feminine archetype of holiness, and could be simply renamed "The Holy Woman". She also holds the same scepter as the king, but she holds it in her left hand, which is connected with the right brain (the intuitive and creative side of the brain) and she is holding the eagle in her right hand. Her crown is again conical. The water of life, a symbol of consciousness, flows at her feet.

20. The Cosmic Idiot

The Cosmic Idiot is an archetype that is defined by its fluid reflection of the divine. It incorporates and manifests different aspects of cosmic wisdom and perfection. Jacob Boehme said, "She moves before God only for the purpose of revealing his miracles." In the Indian tradition, this Idiot is spoken of as an "Avatar", a being that emanates from the divine. Self-realized people like the Perfect Idiot or the Holy Idiot strive towards the divine, while this Idiot *is* the divine, over-taken and manifested in physical form. In Hinduism, it is the reincarnation or appearance of God in a body, for example, Krishna is an Avatar of the God Vishnu. In the belief system of Gurdjieff, Jesus Christ plays this role. The saint is self-realized by God's grace, but the Avatar represents a direct incarnation of the cosmic power of the divine.

This principle is found in other belief-systems, too, like the African religion of Voodoo, in which there are several different forms of God, representing "lines or rays of energy" or spirits, manifesting as warrior, magician, fire and power, time or beauty. They are personified versions of God, but their traits are very human, whereas the Hindu Avatar expresses a more idealized and "Godly" manifestation. This comparison is meant to show that this Idiot can have human traits, likes and dislikes, yet be distinctly beyond humanity.

Tarot: The Tarot card of the "High Priestess" in the sequence of the cards should therefore be renamed "Avatar" or "Cosmic Idiot"...

The Priestess is an archetype of the power of self transcendence. She has developed both sides in herself: she emanates the spiritual power and at the same time she is the power of nature with all its wonderful abilities for erotic love, fertility and creativity which are manifested in the cycles of life: birth, growth and death. She symbolizes the creative intelligence of evolution, creating, destroying, loving and playing. Holiness is not beyond life, but is interwoven with life. A human being incorporating the divinity should be aware, that she (or he) isn't separated from the creation but she or he is a co-worker in the evolution of the consciousness of humanity. Note that the "High Priestess" is on a higher stage than the "Hierophant", which often is associated with the Pope.

21. The Unique Idiot

It is evident that "The Magician" (card No. 1) corresponds to the Unique Idiot. He is the master of the elements and roams the infinite. Gurdjieff spoke of God as the "Unique Idiot". "One day when the Idiots were toasted again and Jane Heap was asked to choose her Idiot, she said: 'I'm no Idiot anymore. I have worked through all.' Gurdjieff said: 'What! No Idiot? Everybody is an Idiot. I am Idiot. Even God is Idiot."

If we apply it to humanity, we would find a human being living by the Will of God as represented by the idea of "the Son of God". We all have a spark of this quality in our soul. The great Sufi Al-Halladj once cried out, "Ana'l haqq" or "I am God", and was hanged. Organized religions have traditionally railed against the idea that we are all unique manifestations of the Infinite (or Creative Intelligence, as I call it) because their priests and dogmatic authorities would lose their hold on power – not to mention their jobs… Lastly, as expressed by Ibn Arabi, "God am I."

When we study the ladder of the Idiots we should take to heart Herman Hesse's "Treatises of Steppenwolf", in which it is quoted, "Because no one, not even the idiot, is pleased by the idea that his entire being could be explained by the sum of two or three main elements; it would be hopeless and childish to explain such a differentiated man as Harry with the naïve division of wolf and man. Harry [and every seeker after truth] doesn't consist of two beings but of hundreds or thousands. His life swings (as does the life of every man) not only between two poles, namely the instinctive urge and the spirit, or the holy and the libertine, but it oscillates between thousands, between infinite poles."

6. The Ritual Meal

"This is a ritual which Christ performed, and which I perform here, and afterward someone else will sit in my place and this will go on."
G. I. Gurdjieff[90]

The "Ladder of Reason" cannot be understood fully without the ritual meal of the "Feast of the Idiots" - this point was emphasized by some of Gurdjieff's pupils. This was the reason given when the official Gurdjieff Foundation discontinued it after his death in 1949[91]. But as mentioned, Gurdjieff envisioned that the tradition should go on. I was lucky enough to participate in this ritual with John G. Bennett, who himself had partaken of the ritual with Gurdjieff himself. These meals gave me an idea – a "taste" (pun intended) of how the ritual was performed in Paris. And now, after many years of practicing the ritual meal with various groups, I'm convinced of its value as a tool for self-knowledge.

How do we perform the ritual today?
To perform the ritual today, certain prerequisites have to be met. There must be a leader in the group who is able to conduct the ritual because he or she can best see what's appropriate at any time and sequence of the ritual. There also should be participants who have worked on themselves for sufficient time in order to have developed some of the features mentioned. If you do this with beginners, the ritual is not fruitful - it will simply entertain, insofar as people will become drunk and the ritual will then bring out their "normal" character traits. If you want to create a carousel or an orgy, then invent your own ritual…

Before the toast is given, the spiritual leader of the group gives some explanation to each Idiot. After the toast, he or she relates a teaching story, and asks for someone to "out" himself or herself as this Idiot. This person should be prepared to share a recent observation, or at least a good story, that illustrates the qualities of this Idiot. The group leader is responsible for the flow of the evening, and for creating the correct atmosphere of both chaos and camaraderie, in order to encourage both attentiveness and spontaneity. Participants should be aware of the rhythm of the entire proceeding, because it is not only the toasts themselves, or even the ideas which form the basis of this psychology that bring about insights, it is the experience itself. Also, anyone who dares to create such a ritual meal should have extensive experience in working with people, in order to have developed an acute awareness of how and when people can be "triggered". These moments arise spontaneously, and have the capacity to stimulate moments of insight, enlightenment or deep reflection. Such moments may take any form - whether word, gesture, confrontation, emotional tone, or lack of any of the above. But above all, the group leader must incorporate within himself a deep compassion and respect for the striving of all participants, so that even words or actions of confrontation are accepted from a place of inner quietness, and thus encourage self-observation by all participants.

Based on my experience, I propose the following points as being important for creating the Ritual Meal:

a) In the afternoon prior to the meal, do at least one hour of the Movements or similar physical exercise, in order to create and focus energies and attention.

b) Follow it with a common inner exercise or meditation.

c) Prepare the meal together. All participants assemble or are organized into small groups, slicing meat and cutting vegetables, etc. to prepare the food. This preparation should be seen as an opportunity to become very aware of what one is doing, whether it is to finely dice carrots, to turn on the oven, or to look for the oil. Working with attention gives the food additional energy. Don't talk during this work, except when coordination or information is needed. Organize the schedule to make sure someone is responsible for every part of the meal. For instance, if you want to cook lamb or other meat, or make sure the soup is hot (as opposed to the cold soup served during Gurdjieff's rituals), timing and coordination are needed.

(Note: Borscht can be made either hot or cold. Both are popular variations. In Spain Gazpacho is served cold, too. But I personally appreciate a hot soup…)

d) After the preparation of the food, the tables and the room should be prepared. Clean and set it for a real feast, which indeed this is, with candles and other details that will help to create a very special atmosphere.

e) When everything is set up, give a reading from Gurdjieff's writings or from another teacher of universal wisdom. Play some appropriate music to relax, and to get into the mood of the ritual.

f) Take a short break, during which time those responsible for serving the meal, or at least this part of it, will get everything ready. Use this time to refresh yourself and put on adequate feast clothing.

g) At the agreed-upon time, or at a signal from the servers, everyone gathers at the table. I usually open the meal with the "remembrance" of John G. Bennett[92] and the ritual begins. Usually we start to eat the salad. When the leader thinks the time is right, he sets the tone. He/she may speak about the first Idiot or start with some other important idea. I sometimes toast first on the creative abundance of Life, because otherwise we wouldn't be here. When the toast is given, all participants repeat it in unison. (For this first Idiot, attention is usually drawn to any children in the group, if present, or to a younger newcomer.) But you can also choose to start with another toast if you think that it fits the moment. For example, during a ritual meal I performed in commemoration of Gurdjieff's birthday (January 13th), we began with a toast to him.

The Toasts are given in order, with teaching stories, personal stories and responses proceeding through to the 12th Idiot (any further Idiots are generally irrelevant to the participants at hand). Throughout the meal, the Director may give other toasts which seem fitting, for example, to an honored guest or to Life, or whatever he/she wants to draw attention to at that moment. The Server is responsible for the drinks and must vigilantly replenish glasses with water or vodka, the only beverages served, while another person is responsible for lighting cigarettes (as mentioned, good tobacco smoke is food for the spirits – shamans still use it until today) and another for passing food. Keep in mind that while these people had special names in Gurdjieff's school, for our purposes the names and even their duties are not that important. We don't want to imitate, but rather explore a ritual process. We are more interested in looking at the dynamics of the development of a ritual feast.

h) The timing of the meal: it is important to develop a menu with several courses. Don't put all the food on the tables at once, but rather spread them out over time. First you will only serve the salad. If the leader thinks it is time, the soup will then be served to a queue, or by passing it along the tables. Later on, the main dish is served, also from the kitchen, and the plates are passed around the circle. If possible, keep the food warm in the kitchen if there is enough for second helpings. You'll end with a dessert, eventually followed by coffee and tea. When the ritual comes to an end, the leader should terminate it with some final words.

i) During the meal itself, don't make small talk. Discuss only relevant topics or insights, or questions and philosophical themes that arise through the progression of the Idiots. As each Toast is given, participants should try to feel the essence of each Idiot. For those that have chosen an Idiot for themselves, they should feel especially deeply, and should share a story from his/her own personal experience that exemplifies this idiocy, while being attentive to the fact that this is an exercise in "self remembering", not "self presentation". The leader, and *only* the leader, can respond to the participants. The leader may, from time to time, allow further discussion, but he or she must be on the alert for the dilution of energy through conversation. The response afforded by the leader can be the most difficult and creative part of the ritual, and requires much sensitivity and skill. He or she should be conscious of the "vibrations" of the group and of the ritual to be able to recognize and even trigger moments that can further the insights and enhance attention. The leader of the group must have the capacity to direct the Ritual with both intention and subtlety. To effectively manage the energies of such a group is not a skill that can be "learned" through the intellect, but rather comes from years of life experience.

j) It is important that everybody remain focused on the topic at hand – the performing of a ritual meal that can lead to personal insights. It wouldn't be relevant or valuable to the meal to have idle talk about jobs or relationships, etc. Feasting together is a joyous occasion, but a certain reverence and sense of aim is needed, so remain aware of when you are adding to the mood, or detracting from it. That said everybody should be prepared to tell a joke. It is an invaluable skill to learn to observe oneself, others, and the moment, while not taking any of it too seriously. In the wisdom of the Three Stooges, "There is a time and place for all things. This is not one of them." But you also can talk about some philosophical ideas of "The Work", this often, because of the heightened awareness, helps to understand some idea deeper.

j) If the ritual during the evening has managed to build up a certain quality and amount of energy and attention, it is advisable not to take a break, for fear of losing continuity. It can diminish the energy field built up during the meal. I think after about minimum of two hours (depending on the group size it can last up to four hours) the leader should close the ritual "officially", letting it end intentionally and summarily, instead of letting the energy wither away. Afterwards people can sit around, drink wine and talk, as desired, or meditate, if still able…

That which has the capacity to open the non-verbal parts of our understanding is difficult, by definition, to explain with words. However, here is an attempt: "The point is that this notion of dialogue and common consciousness suggests that there is some way out of our collective difficulties. If we can all suspend carrying out our impulses, suspend our assumptions and look at them, then we are all in the same state of consciousness. In dialogue the whole structure of defensiveness and opinions and divisions collapse; and suddenly the feeling can change to one of fellowship and friendship, participation and sharing. We are then partaking of the common consciousness." (David Bohm). In this sense: see the Ritual Feast also as a Dialogue.

A feast is a feast – don't make it too serious!

7. "A Toast to the Realized Idiot..."

"Everything which ever came from God is determined to enfold his being by his works in pure form. The characteristic activities for human beings are loving and cognizing. Now the question arises: which of both contains a blessing? Some masters taught it lies in cognition; others state, it lies in loving. Others say the blessing lies both in love and cognition. But I state, the blessing consists neither of cognition nor of love, but there is a something in the soul, from which cognition and love are derived. It itself neither cognizes nor loves - as the powers of the soul do. Only he who recognizes this something can grasp what the blessing consists of. It is without determination or direction, so that it doesn't know that God works in it. Yeah, it is so much itself that it enjoys the same way God enjoys."
Meister Eckhart (1320)

"How can anyone possibly make use of such a science?" This was the reaction of a pupil of Gurdjieff's when I asked him to elaborate on the teaching of the Idiots. I was surprised at the harshness of the response, but it remains an example of the attitude that prevails amongst some "traditionalists", who seek a museum-like preservation of Gurdjieff's teaching. It is evident that his "Science of Idiotism" has a teaching value; else he would not have introduced and practiced it for decades. And if it cannot work without a "master", then a "master" is what we must become.

Any philosopher, spiritual teaching, or spiritual master can only show the *relative* truth of things. And every teaching always embodies the individual form and understanding of the teacher. Lastly, the teacher is human. Objective truth doesn't exist because the human mind cannot be objective, nor can there be any "objective thing" in the universe. We are. The universe is. Or maybe it isn't. Perhaps this is all an illusion of the mind, *maya*, as the Indian philosophy suggests.

A list of 21 Idiots is naturally limited and even arbitrary. If we observe the many different people we meet during our life - and especially the people who undertake a spiritual journey - we will certainly find many other Idiots or variations of Idiots. I could imagine an "Incorrigible Idiot" or a "Know-it-all Idiot" or a "Clever Idiot". The poet Elias Canetti describes fifty characters,[93] some of which could be qualified as Idiots, like "Name Taster" or "The Ear Witness", a type which doesn't look at things, but hears everything... The characteristics and weaknesses are legion. But while studying the Idiot types more deeply by yourself, you will discover that many of the other Idiots you can name are contained in one or another of Gurdjieff's Idiots. Of course, these variations don't diminish the necessity for methods and teachings that help us on our journey to self-knowledge.

As we are born into a world of limitations, we have forgotten our limitlessness. We have become socialized, and now fit into some relation to society, we have submitted ourselves to the laws of the market, built up an acceptable personality to get on with others who themselves have created acceptable personalities. If we don't succeed at this, we are bound to live on the fringe of society or become eccentric. These mechanisms of adaptation go unnoticed, until one day we see through them. Even then it is not easy to separate from these mechanisms, which bind us to certain patterns of behavior and offense. In Gurdjieff's *Beelzebub's Tales*, Beelzebub becomes upset with his grandson, Hassein, for calling human beings "slugs". He said humans are easily insulted, and the situation would surely come to blows. He explained to his grandson that people take "imagination for reality". "This strange trait of their general psyche, namely, of being satisfied with just what Smith or Brown says, without trying to know more, became rooted in them already long ago, and now they no longer strive at all to know anything cognizable by their own active deliberations alone.

"Concerning all this it must be said that neither the organ Kundabuffer which their ancestors had is to blame, nor its consequences which, owing to a mistake on the part of certain Sacred Individuals, were crystallized in their ancestors and later began to pass by heredity from generation and generation.

"But they themselves were personally to blame for it, and just on account of the abnormal conditions of external ordinary being-existence which they themselves have gradually established and which have gradually formed in their common presence just what has now become their inner 'Evil-God', called 'Self-Calming'."[94]

Of course we feel insulted when the weaknesses in our character are pointed out. Who wants to be told that he is an "Idiot" – even jokingly? In general, we *are* idiots, in the contemporary meaning of the word. Even worse, we are primarily "conceited idiots". It may actually make sense that a word that originally meant "private" or "special" individual came to have a derogatory meaning. A person who has found a way to self-perfection may have also found just enough rope to hang themselves. The temptation to feel "more special than others", as does the "Enlightened Idiot", is both ironic and overwhelming. "The path of knowledge leads only to the stage of the Enlightened Idiot. Of this Mr. Gurdjieff spoke sometimes in scorn but more often in deep compassion. 'I pity Enlightened Idiot. More unhappy person not exist... No-one can help him. Not even God can help him'. The terrible situation of the Enlightened Idiot disturbed many people profoundly, and Mr. Gurdjieff was frequently asked whether there was really no possible way out. Sometimes he replied that if such an Idiot came to him and could pay enough, he could perhaps help him. But then he would have to descend all the way back to Ordinary Idiot and start afresh. This was very difficult: he would have to give up all that he had gained from so much labor. But if he had the courage to do so, he would be able to ascend consciously from Ordinary Idiot, and this time he could pass through Enlightened Idiot and reach Number Seventeen."[95]

To reach an understanding of our essence, we must first learn to be an "Ordinary Idiot", which means to have the capacity for honest self-reflection without self-calming or self-deception. This is a very prickly idea to vanity, which does not want to be "ordinary", nor an "idiot", and certainly not an "ordinary idiot" (though, maybe a fantastic one!). "Besides this chief particularity of their common psyche, there are completely crystallized in them and there unfailingly become part of their common presences - regardless of where they may arise and exist - functions which exist under the names 'egoism', 'self-love', 'vanity', 'pride', 'self-conceit', 'credulity', 'suggestibility', and many other properties quite abnormal and quite unbecoming to the essence of any three-brained beings whatsoever."[96]

It is not really astonishing that peculiarities, ranging from vanity to gullibility, often thrive in the Petri dish of spiritual following. People believe most in things that they can in no way prove or test, and that lie furthest from them - from invisible masters to extraterrestrial beings. A lot of candidates for the madhouse collect in the so-called "marketplace of the esoteric". This is an important reason to make Gurdjieff's teaching and especially the "Science of Idiotism" known. I think that the thought alone that one is an "Idiot" is very helpful when one follows a certain spiritual path, because it invites humor and humility, and makes the path and goal relative. We can always say to ourselves, "What an Idiot I am!" and mean it. The ancient Egyptian god, Thoth, was the god of wisdom in the form of a monkey, showing the long tradition of blending wisdom and humor – because only through humor can wisdom keeps itself in perspective! In general, that which is closest to us is over-looked. We become involved with "enlightened" philosophies and lose contact with basic realities. The "Science of Idiotism" is a hint to get back down to earth, and to not start a war over a monkey!

Through this text, I'm not trying to propagate an ultimate truth. An intelligent teaching should rather show the human weaknesses and special characteristics that are hindrances to our becoming more aware of any potential truth out there. It should be a sword to cut away the chaff. And it should be a toolbox, providing the necessary tools for working on oneself. The genius mystic Meister Eckhart said in the 14th century that the aim of our search should be to become "poor in spirit", which means to empty oneself of all preconceived beliefs and ideas. "Therefore I ask God that he should relieve me of God, as my essential being is beyond God if we understand God as the origin of the species. Because in the same origin of God which was the cause that God stands above, of being and difference, there I was myself. There I wanted myself and there I recognized myself as the one who created this human being. Therefore I am the origin of myself, after my being which is eternal, and not after my becoming which is in time."[97]

In summary, we create our reality and ourselves. We must aim to integrate and transform the parts into a whole and to "become oneself". Therefore, to my eyes, Gurdjieff's teaching is a springboard from which to step beyond one's biases and pre-conceived notions. Nevertheless, it is difficult to leave behind the identification with dualism of a material and spiritual world, although we have seen through it with all its traps. It is a paradox - as long we are walking "on the path" we *remain* on the path, and when we stop searching, we are found. Gurdjieff emphasized that the "higher centers" are already fully developed, and that the means for cognition and love are already inside of us. But we block our own path (pun intended). To break through to these divine qualities, this place of miracles, we must become "poor in spirit", and empty ourselves of everything that is not "essential". Imagine a door that is so narrow that only you can fit, but your luggage, consisting of your false personality, your identification and self-deception, all your lies, opinions and beliefs, is too big and has to be left outside. It doesn't really matter which master we follow, or which truth we find for ourselves, the main issue remains the same; we are stubborn bastards. This is the teaching of Gurdjieff's "Science of Idiotism". We are ourselves the greatest hindrances to our own unfolding, and we put up a wall at the threshold of our freedom, by following a teaching instead of really working. Nobody can free or redeem us, this is something we can only do ourselves. We have to grasp our original ability to know what we already know.

The great Sufi Hazrat Inayat Khan reminds us of this simple wisdom, "Trust your first intuition." If we free ourselves from doubts, deceptions and everything that obstructs our view of the great wilderness (reality), we will have the intuition, knowledge and insight necessary to move forward. The great thinkers always emphasized: "Know yourself". In the language of Meister Eckhart, "There I am neither God nor creature, yes, there I am that what I ever was and will be, now and forever."

Appendix

Some notes to the meaning and history of the Tarot

A person who had a mastery of language was able get in touch with the gods, or report about their deeds. The early shamans, tens of thousands of years ago, already knew songs for calling the higher powers (also called "spirits") or energies of life, if they worked themselves into higher or enhanced states of consciousness. It is still a mystery how the early humans, some hundred thousands of years ago, developed language at all. As we know from stories about wolf children (children who were reared by wolves), or the famous Kaspar Hauser story in Germany, children cannot learn to speak effectively unless they start learning in infancy, or at least with great difficulties as the ability obviously is put in our cells.

So the mystery of the acquisition of language has been an instrument of power for the priests of old ages, because if you could call things by their names you will have power over them – an important experience for humanity. The first act of Adam in the Hebrew creation myth is the naming of plants and animals.

The old Egyptian culture is saturated with the idea of making connections with the gods by means of "words of power". The priests are said to have been able to bring the gods to life with these words. Many graves of priests and kings were filled with scriptures and paintings, and very often the dead were given texts from the "Egyptian Book of the Dead", which were intended to ensure that the deceased would have a good journey into the next world.

The songs of the shamans or the recitations of the old Indian Vedas are grounded in the concept that words are tools for connecting with the spirits or gods.

Words of power were not only used by priests, but also by doctors and healers. For a very long time, both of these professions – priest and doctor – were one. A shaman travels into another world either to gain insight or the ability to heal, or to bring back a formula for the appropriate drug to use. Another aim for travelling into the realm of the spirits is to see in what way the fabric or web of the soul of a patient is broken, and to enlist the help or gather the energy needed to repair the mesh of soul and body.

When humanity developed scripture and writing, pictures or written characters were sufficient to mend the fabric of the soul. Therefore, these pictures or characters were applied to the graves. The Egyptians painted their pictures on the walls, in the expectation that the dead person would be carried on a boat into the immortal afterlife. Amulets or other magical objects are still in use today for the same purpose: a call for help to the spirits.

"Magical" or in other words "effective" words have always been of significant value to the people. Just think of the politicians who must still give public speeches to convince people to elect them. Although the information about their aspirations is available everywhere in written form, yet they must still give speeches to impart the same information. A good speech can make the difference – best example today is Barack Obama. I will speak later on about the connection of words with the Tarot.

The basic idea and conception of the Tarot very probably came from the Egyptian Book of Thoth, but it also could come from the Indus scripture via the Phoenicians. The connection with old India is well possible. Thoth was the god of science and wisdom, and had the head of a monkey. In India we find the same god of wisdom, who there is called Hanuman, and is also represented as a monkey. Anyway the pictures of the tarot came to the European continent across the Mediterranean Sea.

Maybe one has accounted the Egypt's with there hieroglyphic pictures for it, as with all fascinating things, the Egyptian Book of Thoth is clouded in mystery. It is said that it was hidden in an iron-clad box. This box was contained in a bronze box, which in turn was situated in a box of palm wood, which in its turn again had been put into a box of ebony and ivory. This box, further, was inside a silver box and that one, finally, had been put into a golden box. The whole sequence of boxes was surrounded by snakes and scorpions and a big snake, which patrolled ceaselessly, and which was unable to be killed by any weapon.

This allegory shows that even for the Egyptians, the mystery of wisdom was inaccessible. The book was protected on seven layers, which hints at the seven different states of consciousness or understanding which have been written about in many esoteric teachings. Therefore, we still speak of the "seven seals of wisdom". The so-called "Seal of Thoth" we find again in the Tarot card of "The World" which is also shown again in Gurdjieff's emblem of his "Institute for the Harmonious Development of Man". An illustration of the same things, especially the four figures at the corners, can also be found in the biblical story of Hezekiah. Read the story (especially Hezekiah 1)!

In this biblical story, he has a vision of a figure with four faces, of an eagle, a bull, a lion and a human. This figure talks to Hezekiah, and it is interesting to note that he (in the end he saw the Lord) gave him a scroll to eat. "Then I ate it and it was sweet as honey." After he ate it, he was directed to speak to the Israelites. The symbolic presentation of the four animals is again described in the Book of Revelation. The Egyptian Sphinx statue, which protects the secret, is also designed to show four animals and a woman's head, similar to the Tarot card "The World".

How can it be proven that the idea of the Tarot comes from the Book of Thoth? Thoth, in the Egyptian tradition, is the master of words. His magical formulas are the basis of the secret wisdom.

Thoth is always seen as the transmitter of creative language. All wisdom and knowledge have their source in a monkey god – maybe reminiscent of the evolution of human beings from apes. But Thoth is also the symbol of deeper knowledge. Only those who are able to connect the ideas which are expressed by letters, numbers and pictures, can use the power which they symbolise.

The old Egyptians had three forms of script: hieroglyphs (holy signs), a hieratic (shorthand) script (which resembles handwriting) and a later addition – the so-called demotic script (which resembles stenography). The Arabic characters probably evolved from this script. The hieroglyphs were used in several ways: as signs for words (ideograms), as signs for sounds (phonograms) and as determinatives. Ideograms express a picture of the object or being illustrated, without reference to the sound. Chinese script is a similar form – the same character can be associated with many (sometimes quite different) sounds, which are the 'dialects' assigned to them in different regions of China. For an action, the hieroglyph would represent a verb, and such pictures were also used. Very early on, the Egyptians, instead of a term (which may be difficult to express in an appropriate picture) started to use a phonetic sound associated with a picture, and which sound was in fact not related at all to the actual item being represented (as in Japanese, too). That is the same as if we were to use a picture of heaven for the term "heaven". Then there are signs (characters) for consonants, which result in a word without vowels. Sometimes, ideograms and phonograms were even combined. In this way, many texts were composed in pictorial puzzles.

The fascination with the hieroglyphic pictorial puzzle – the precursor of the later alphabetical script – is the possibility of expressing ideas through a combination of symbols, or simply to illustrate letters. As the Egyptian language is part of the Semitic language group, it is no wonder that the letters of the Hebrew alphabet express the threefold characteristics of picture, number and sign (ideogram). This is something of which typical modern Israelis are no longer aware. This threefold characteristic of symbol (or picture), number and sign is something which we find again in the Tarot.

It is not known how the Tarot we know today originated and who developed it. Historically, we only know that it emerged in the 14th century, at a time when the Christian kings were repelling the Muslims in Spain. The Tarot deck of 22 cards, called the Greater Arcane - (arcane being translated as secret, but which may also have been derived from the Arabic word *arkan*, element) - surfaced as the Moors were evacuating Granada in 1491. The Moors and Muslims had been the guarantors of the security of the Jews, who as believers with a revealed book had been tolerated by Islamic authorities. The Book of Illumination, called Zohar, was also written in the 13th century, and was disseminated in the 14th century. The Gypsies, who are said to have propagated the Tarot, only became known in Europe after the Tarot had already been disseminated widely. However, as travelling trades-persons, they contributed substantially to its propagation, especially by means of fortune telling.

We can assume that the Tarot developed as the result of a cooperation of the Spanish Sufis and the Jewish cabalists, and that its aim was the safeguarding of the esoteric tradition in the West. Of course, it did not encompass the entire corpus of then-known knowledge, but should rather be considered as an action implementation for the spiritual development within the European Christian community, which lost a considerable volume of cultural and philosophical knowledge during its fight against Islam. Both groups must have been interested in encrypting or ciphering (a word which stems from the cabalistic word "sefer" - book) their knowledge in a secure way, in order to survive the Spanish *reconquista*. Nobody at this time (shortly after the crusades), could know which books and information would be able to survive in Europe. But pictures and playing cards always circulate among the people (even today in Iran or other Islamic countries, where they are forbidden), and such cards are always suitable for containing encrypted information or messages.

The Tarot most probably reached Italy from Spain and in the beginning, the Italians called it *attuti*. This word expresses, without doubt, an Italian echo of the Hebrew word *Autiot* – which is the name for Hebrew script signs. At the same time, the Renaissance commenced in Italy, and the banker Cosimo de Medici founded his Neo-Platonist Academy, where the entire knowledge of the old Greek philosophers and all extant knowledge was restored and taught.

Another possibility for understanding the background of the Tarot is to decipher the word Tarot by means of its letters and numbers. We must understand that each Hebrew letter is also a number. Since in Hebrew (as in Arabic) only consonants (i.e. the roots of the words) are written, the word Tarot can be built up from T-R-T (the vowels are not written). In Hebrew this is Tet, Resh, Tav. So we have three words: Tet is the also number 9 and has the meaning of cell, building block (or alphabetic character); the word Resh signifies the number 200 with the meaning of universe, unity, and the word Tav, number 400, has the meaning of collection, reservoir – it also is used as the conclusion of the sequence of letters and is a complement to Aleph, the first letter.

So, if we translate the word "Tarot" with these meanings, we will arrive at "the collected building blocks (or cells) of the universe." Building blocks can also substitute for, or mean "elements", therefore "Arcane".

Now we still have the riddle of the origin of the pictures. Some authors suggest that the pictures of the Tarot, as they were disseminated in the West, in fact originate from the Book of Thoth, which was written in hieroglyphs on the walls of the Temple of Initiation at Memphis. Authors such as Enel, Court de Geblin, Luginbühl and others present Egyptian images from this book which corresponds to the later images of the Tarot. These pictures were reconstructions based on of descriptions by Appolonius of Tyana and/or the philosophical writings of Ramon Llull of Mallorca. It is most probable that the old hieroglyphic images were taken as blueprints for the known pictures of the Tarot, as the mythical and archetypal images were a cultural treasure or even folklore in the middle Ages. The Renaissance painter Andrea Mantegna painted a sequence of these images, which are contained in the Tarot cards called "The Tarot de Marseilles", used in this book.

The spiritual leaders of humanity have always tried to secure the knowledge or wisdom of their time by means diverse coded measurements, or to transmit it in a way that people could understand. The Jewish Kabbalah developed only around the turn of the first century, and until then was transmitted only orally. However, it is believed to date back to the time of Moses, who was in turn an initiate of the Egyptian mysteries. The main cabbalistic books which contain "cosmic wisdom" are the *Sefer Yetzira*, the *Sefer ha Zohar* and the *Clavigula* (the little keys) of Salomon. The Clavigula consisted of figures which corresponded to the hieroglyphic signs of the Tarot. It is said that this scripture is registered in the National Library of Paris (I couldn't verify this personally). The *Sefer Yetzira* originated between the third and the sixth century; the other scriptures some hundred years later.

The Jewish Kabbalah, which in diverse forms has influenced Western thinking for centuries, has a parallel in the Science of Letters of the Sufis called *ilm-i-abjad*. There, a consonant is also identified with a number. It is difficult to say whether both stem from the same source – but it is known that the Prophet

Mohammad did learn from Jewish masters and some *Sura* of the *Qur'an* begin with initial letters which hint at the hidden meaning of the following text.

Ernest Scott in his work *The People of the Secret* writes that the Kabbalah is an amalgam of two old traditions, "Two separate but similar expressions of an old objective science came together as completely oral transmissions and later were written down as a code." The new version mysteriously emerged in the West around the year 1000. Where did it originate? It would be unbelievable if it had not been a Jewish source but a Sufic one. The acknowledged Jewish Encyclopaedia explains that the Kabbalah originated in Basra as the Work "Encyclopaedia of the Pure Brethren" published in 980. It is in fact possible that the cabbalistic wisdom was taken into account by the esoteric group of the encyclopaedists, but the Kabbalah has its initial roots in the writings of the Torah, and therefore with Genesis, the Book of Creation, which is already an encrypted book. If it were not so, we would not have been able to decipher it subsequently and make sense of the deciphering. The term "Tarot", of course, has a parallel in the term "Torah". In Tarot the letter Tet is simply substituted for the letter He. The letter or sign He has the meaning of breath, and hints at a revelation, while the letter Tet has the meaning of collection, which could also be an encyclopaedia, a collection of knowledge.

Little is known about the brethren of Basra, although the philosophical-mathematical work *Kitab Ikhwan as-safa* (with *safa* we have again *sefer*, cipher) was the basic study material of the later Sufi mystics and authors such as Ibn Arabi and Al Ghasali. This work became famous not only because of its contents, but because of the mystery of the anonymity which surrounded it. One of my suppositions is that the encyclopaedists of Basra were a branch or perhaps even the main center of the mysterious Sarmoun-Brotherhood, of which Gurdjieff and later on Idries

Shah spoke. Sarmoun (or Sarman) can be translated as "Guardians of the Tradition" and Kabbalah also means "tradition" – transmission of knowledge. Do we have here an important key? Whether the "Science of the Idiots" is derived from the Greater Arcane of the Tarot is something I am unable to prove. But, as we have seen, there are manifold parallels and correspondences. And in the Tarot, we can find a connectivity of the spiritual and psychological wisdom of all times: "As above, so below."

The real knowledge in fact is never hidden, it can be found by every "Searcher for the Truth", as Gurdjieff called his group when he made his explorations in Asia. But always, there is a natural barrier which ensures that uninitiated people without adequate training or effort are not able to access the key to the secrets. The Tarot is a building block to the understanding of cosmic interrelationships and the development of humans, and if you look with open eyes you will also see and feel the guidance which has been offered to humanity at all times. The more we are able to use this knowledge correctly and responsibly, and for the benefit of humanity, the more will be revealed. But knowledge and wisdom are not free: we must work for them by "conscious labour and intentional suffering" as Gurdjieff put it.

Note of Thanks

Although I am solely responsible for the content and conclusions of this book, many people have helped me to understand these ideas and put them down on paper. To all those who have helped me either directly or indirectly, I offer my sincerest gratitude.

It was J. G. Bennett through whom I originally came into contact with the practical and theoretical teachings of G.I. Gurdjieff. Thanks to his initiative, people continue to this day to think about and research these ideas independently, ensuring that it doesn't crystallize into dead words and stagnant form. One of these people is Anthony G. E. Blake, who always inspired me to new vistas and encouraged me to write this book, which seemed somehow impossible in the beginning.

But finally I wouldn't have written this book had it not been for the encouragement of my wife, Nana Nauwald. She supported my plans and lovingly strengthened my resolve to research the Idiots, despite the overwhelming dogma declaring the "Science of Idiotism" as "taboo". Her creative insights helped to formulate innovative ideas and terms that aren't found in Gurdjieff-related literature.

I give many thanks to my American editor Pippa Arend. She was able to put my text into a readable American version and helped me to clarify many things that I hadn't considered. Also thanks to Mike Krochmal, a German-Australian, who helped to improve it a bit more.

I believe John G. Bennett would have encouraged me to write this book, as he always was very open to genuine new thoughts and ideas. In 1973, after I returned to Germany from his Academy in Sherborne, I asked him if I could publish his books. Although I was not a publisher at this time and did not have any experience, he ventured, "Just go on!" For him, it was the spirit of experiment and adventure that was important – the potential of an undertaking and the risk of failure, without which nothing creative can be achieved.

Bibliography

Anirvan, Sri and Lizelle Reymond: To Live Within, Masham, New Yorkshire, 1984

Bennett, John G.: Gurdjieff - Making a New World, Santa Fe, 1992

Bennett, John G.: Deeper Man, Santa Fe, 1994

Bennett, John G.: A Spiritual Psychology, Santa Fe, 1999

Bennett, John G.: Seven Lines of Work, Claymont, 1979

Bennett, John G.: Sacred Influences, Santa Fe, 1989

Bennett, John G.: The Science of Idiotism, unpublished Manuscript, 1950

Bennett, John G.: The Psychological Basis, in: Systematics, Vol. 4, No. 4 (1967)

Bennett, John G.: The Way to be Free, New York, 1980

Bennett, John G.: Witness, Santa Fe, 1997

Bennett, John G.: Elementary Systematics, Santa Fe, 1993

Bennett, Elizabeth: Idiots in Paris, York Beach, 1991

Bennet, John G.: The Dramatic Universe, 4 Vol.

Blake, Anthony G. E.: The Intelligent Enneagram, Boston, 1996

Blake, Anthony G. E.: The Supreme Art of Dialogue - Structures of Meaning, Charles Town, 2008

Blake, Anthony G. E.: An Index to In Search of the Miraculous, Charles Town, 1982

Boorstein, Seymour (ed.): Transpersonal Psychotherapy, 1980

Collin, Rodney: The Theory of Celestial Influences, London, 1980

Friedlander, Joel: Body Types - The Enneagram of Essence Types, New York, 1993

Gurdjieff, G.I.: Beelzebubs Tales to His Grandson, London, 1950

Guide and Index to Gurdjieff's All and Everything, Toronto, 1973

Gurdjieff, G.I.: Meetings with Remarkable Men, New York, 1969

Gurdjieff, G.I.: Life is Real Only Then, when "I AM", New York

Gurdjieff, G.I.: Views from the Real World, London, 1973

Gurdjieff Everitt, Luba: A Memoir with Recipes, Berkeley, 1993

Hands, Rina: Diary of Madame Egout Pour Sweet, Aurora, 1991

Hesse, Hermann: Steppenwolf, Pinguin Books, 2007

Kaplan, Stuart R.: The Encyclopaedia of the Tarot, New York, 1978

Levy, Eliphas: Der Schlüssel zu den großen Mysterien, Weilheim, 1966

Martin, Bruno: Auf einem Raumschiff mit Gurdjieff, Norderstedt, 2009

Martin, Bruno: Das Lexikon der Spiritualität, München, 2005

Martin, Bruno: Intelligente Evolution, München, 2007

Meister Eckhart: The Sermons and Collations of Meister Eckhart (Kessinger Publishing's Rare Reprints), 2005, and other collections like Tractates of Meister Eckhart.

Moore, James: Gurdjieff - The Anatomy of a Myth, Shaftesbury, 1991

Naranjo, Claudio: Enneatypes in Psychotherapy, Hohm Press, 1995

Nicoll, Maurice: Psychological Commentaries of Gurdjieff & Ouspensky, 5 Vol., London, 1952

Nott, C.S. Teachings of Gurdjieff, London, 1961

Nott, C.S. Journey through this World, London, 1969

Ouspensky, P.D.: In Search of the Miraculous, New York, 1977

Ouspensky, P.D.: The Fourth Way, New York, 1971

Palmer, Helen: The Enneagram, New York, 1991

Scott, Ernest: The People of the Secret, London, 1983

Shah, Idries: Wisdom of the Idiots, London, 1991

Shah, Idries: The Pleasantries of the Incredible Mulla Nasrudin, London, 1968

Shah, Idries: The Sufis, London, 1999

Stuart, Micheline, The Tarot - Path to Self-Development, Boulder 1977

Zuber, René: Who are you, Monsieur Gurdjieff? 1980

Notes

1 There is controversy about the date of his birth, but I think that logically it must have been around 1866.

2 John G. Bennett, Making of a New World, (place, see bibliography, also further quotations of books) p. 158

3 Therefore I don't give the original source books in a footnote. Another reason is that very often one reads such a story, remembers it and without making a note somewhere, you will never find it again…

4 P. D. Ouspensky: In Search of the Miraculous, Orlando FL (Harcourt Brace Jovanovich, 1977) (shortened in further quotations: ISM), p. 281

5 See: John G. Bennett: The Masters of Wisdom, Bennett Books, Santa Fe, 1995

6 J. G. Bennett, Making a New World, p. 6

7 See: Bessermann/Steger: Crazy Clouds, Zen Radicals, Rebels & Reformers, Shambala Publications, Boston, 1991

8 See Inazo Nitobe: Bushido, Kodansha Intl., 2002

9 See my exercise book „Gurdjieff Praxisbuch", Darmstadt, 2008, only in German yet.

10 See John G. Bennett: Energies, Sherborne 1975

11 There are several books reporting about this time. For me C. S. Nott: "Teachings of Gurdjieff – The Journal of a Pupil" gives a manifold insight into the work at the Prieuré.

12 ISM, p. 39

13 Says Solange Claustres, a long time pupil, in her memoirs.

14 Bennett, Witness (see bibliography)

15 Witness p. 266

16 See ISM p. 30-31

17 Witness, p. 258

18 J. G. Bennett: Witness, p. 263

19 Narrated by D. T. Suzuki

20 Rina Hands, Madame Egout pour Sweet, p. 33

21 See my book: Intelligente Evolution, München 2007

22 John G. Bennett, Intimations, p. 58

23 J.G. Bennett, A Way to be Free, p. 133

24 Rina Hands, p. 2

25 G. I. Gurdjieff: Beelzebub Tales to his Grandson, p. 143-44

26 CDs with the book about the history of the records have now been published by Basta Music, Netherlands: Gurdjieff: Harmonic Development – The complete Harmonium Recordings 1948-1949, compiled and produced by G. J. Blom.

27 Quoted in this book, p. 20

28 Rina Hands, p. 4

29 E. Bennett, p. ix

30 Luba Gurdjieff: A Memoir with Recipes, p. 81

31 Luba Gurdjieff, A Memoir with Recipes, p. 81

32 Luba Gurdjieff: Memoir with Recipes, op. cit.

33 Rina Hands, p. 5

34 See Anthony Blake: The Intelligent Enneagram, Boston 1996

35 Kenneth Walker, Venture with Ideas, p. 141

36 See her paintings on www.visionary-art.de (with English part)

37 J. G. Bennett, Deeper Man, p. 196

38 In: Views of the Real World, p. 281

39 C. S. Nott, Teachings of Gurdjieff

40 James Moore, Gurdjieff, p. 355

41 Helen Palmer, Enneagram

42 For the whole concept of Psychosynthesis see Seymour Boorstein (ed.): Transpersonal Psychotherapy (Science and Behaviour Books, Inc., 1980), article of John Firman and James Vargiu "Personal and Transpersonal Growth". Psychosynthesis was founded by the Italian Roberto Assagioli (1888-1974), who was the first Western psychologist to seriously incorporate religion and spirituality into an overall view of the human psyche.

43 For a definition of character see further in the text.

44 An idea from Anthony G. E. Blake, a pupil of J. G. Bennett.

45 ISM, p. 162/63

46 In: Views from the Real World – Early Talks of Gurdjieff, London 1973 (Routledge & Kegan Paul Ltd), p. 143

47 Ouspensky, op. cit., p. 163

48 See J. G. Bennett: Deeper Man, Santa Fe 1994

49 Bennett distinguishes between a material self, a reactional self, a divided self and a true self. The divided self as part of the whole self therefore is our character, both conscious and unconscious.

50 John G. Bennett, A Spiritual Psychology, Santa Fe 1999, p. 149

51 John G. Bennett, A Spiritual Psychology, Santa Fe 1999, p. 149

52 See Amit Goswami: The Conscious Universe. The "ego" in this context relates to the personality.

53 J.G.Bennett, Deeper Man, p. 81

54 See Gerald Hüther: Die Macht der inneren Bilder, Göttingen 2006, p. 16

55 Views from the Real World, p. 143

56 See Boorstein, Footnote 3

57 ISM, p. 251-3. Gurdjieff indeed mentions "narcotics" as a mean of separation, and the crave for sweets is typical of the use of hashish; see ISM, op. cit., p. 162

58 ISM, p. 163

59 Maurice Nicoll, p. 511

60 Annie Lou Staveley (1906-1996) lived in England for more than 30 years, and it was there that she met P.D. Ouspensky, and then Jane Heap, with whom she studied the ideas of Gurdjieff in preparation for the moment at the end of the Second World War, when she and her fellow pupils traveled to Paris to study under Mr. Gurdjieff himself. She eventually moved to rural Oregon and started a community named Two Rivers Farm

61 David Kherdian: On a spaceship with Beelzebub

62 ISM p. 267

63 Maurice Nicoll, p. 508

64 Notes of Jane Heap

65 C. S. Nott: Journey Through This World, London 1969, p. 87

66 According to your Real I, your individual pattern of acting.

67 René Zuber, Qui êtes-vous Monsieur Gurdjieff. From the author: I have quoted rather extensively in this chapter, as it helps to understand how Gurdjieff used the Science. Through the memories of the people who experienced him, one can better get a feel for it.

68 E. Bennett, Idiots in Paris, p. 83

69 E. Bennett: Idiots in Paris, p. ix

70 Bennett, Making a new world, p. 157-8

71 Not all of the names of the Idiots are transmitted or can be found in literature. Also I have adapted some names to their significant meanings and found new names, which seemed for me logical in the gradation of reason.

72 J. G. Bennett, unpublished manuscript, all following quotations (in quotation marks) without numbering are from this manuscript.

73 In many decks in the Tarot (see next passage) "The Fool" is numbered with zero; he's the "joker". So, when I say the sequence from 1 to 10 belongs to the "material essence", the fool is the "Helpful or Ordinary Idiot" symbolizing a way to get back to "one's senses", to real essence.

74 Micheline Stuart: The Tarot-Way to Self-Development, Boulder, CO, 1977. M. Stuart was a student of Maurice Nicoll.

75 Quoted in Elizabeth Bennett, Idiots in Paris, op. cit., where he says 4.500 years old. But this is one of Gurdjieff's exaggerations…

76 J. G. Bennett, Way to be Free, p. 151

77 ISM p. 362-365

78 Bennett, Way to be Free, p. 150

79 Rue de Colonel Renard No. 6

80 Retold after a story in: Paul Reps, Without Words, Without Silence.

81 In old Russia the Friday was a free day and a market day. So everybody who had debts to pay promised to pay these at the market. If someone didn't come up people said he "has seven Fridays a week".

82 A term Gurdjieff used in Beelzebub's Tales to describe a whole human being, when all centers are synchronized.

83 J. G. Bennett, unpublished manuscript.

84 Gospel of Thomas

85 Beelzebub, 599 or: Vol.2., p. 192

86 By some reports, a Remorseful Idiot was presented as an Idiot unto itself (or as No. 12), however I am of the opinion that it represents the positive development of any Idiot.

87 See Barbara G. Walker: The Secrets of the Tarot, New York 1985 (Harper & Row)

88 JGB in "Idiots in Paris", p. 38-39

89 JGB, Spiritual Psychology, p. 181

90 quoted in: E. Bennett: Idiots in Paris, p. 59

91 See James Moore: Gurdjieff

92 It goes: „All life is one and everything that lives is holy; plants, animals and humans [to avoid „man]. All have to eat and nourish one another. We thank the life that has given itself so we can live. Let us eat consciously to transform this food into spirit and we therefore close the circle of life by our conscious thoughts, words and deeds." [This is a modified version of the original, which I find more appropriate because it is neutral without any religious connotation. If you wish, you can make it more poetic; or you can use for the last part the original text after "and": "pay back the debts of our existence by our words and deeds."]

93 See Elias Canetti: Earwitness

94 Beelzebub's Tales, p. 104-5

95 J. G. Bennett, The Science of Idiotism, unpublished manuscript.

96 Beelzebub's Tales, p. 107

97 Meister Eckhart in a new German translation, rendered by the author into English.